THE CBT WORKBOOK FOR ANGER MANAGEMENT

THE CBT

WORKBOOK

FOR ANGER

MANAGEMENT

EVIDENCE-BASED EXERCISES
TO HELP YOU UNDERSTAND YOUR TRIGGERS
AND TAKE CHARGE OF YOUR EMOTIONS

NIXALY LEONARDO, LCSW

**ROCKRIDGE
PRESS**

For general information on our other products and services or to obtain technical support, please contact our Customer Care Department within the United States at (866) 744-2665, or outside the United States at (510) 253-0500.

Rockridge Press publishes its books in a variety of electronic and print formats. Some content that appears in print may not be available in electronic books, and vice versa.

TRADEMARKS: Rockridge Press and the Rockridge Press logo are trademarks or registered trademarks of Callisto Media Inc. and/or its affiliates, in the United States and other countries, and may not be used without written permission. All other trademarks are the property of their respective owners. Rockridge Press is not associated with any product or vendor mentioned in this book.

Cover Designer: Angie Chiu
Interior Designer: Carlos Esparza
Art Producer: Maya Melenchuk
Editor: Jed Bickman
Production Editor: Nora Milman
Production Manager: Jose Olivera

Author photo courtesy of Aleksandr Yakubov

Paperback ISBN: 978-1-63807-923-1
eBook ISBN: 978-1-63807-609-4
R0

To my husband: Thank you for holding down the fort while I worked on this book.

And to my preschooler, who sat on my lap coloring and practicing her handwriting while Mama worked on her "really long story."

Contents

Introduction

THIS WORKBOOK HAS BEEN CREATED TO HELP YOU OVERCOME unhealthy anger, using an approach called cognitive behavior therapy (CBT). CBT is a therapeutic approach that I've found to be the most effective in my work as a psychotherapist, helping my clients reach their goals. I even use the techniques on myself. I became a believer in CBT when I was in graduate school and received an assignment to try the techniques out myself. This opportunity to practice CBT techniques demonstrated to me how effective it is, especially for managing anger. Like most people, I feel angry sometimes, and I use CBT techniques to process my anger in a healthy way.

Unhealthy anger ultimately stems from negative thoughts. Negative thoughts can lead to unhealthy coping skills and/or behavioral issues. Because of this, a therapy that focuses on behaviors and thought processes, like CBT, is most appropriate. CBT techniques are helpful for managing anger at any stage, from irritability or annoyance to huge outbursts, and one benefit is that you can begin to see the results right away.

In order to take control over your anger, you'll have to understand it and its effects on you and others in your life. Unhealthy anger is unpleasant, both for the person experiencing it and for those on the receiving end of the interaction. It causes emotional and physical discomfort, self-esteem issues, and relationship problems. It can lead to loneliness, difficulty concentrating, legal problems, and health complications. Because of the impact of unhealthy anger on your life, delving into it might be painful and difficult, but you are not alone in this process. I understand your challenges, and your decision to begin this workbook has put you in the right hands. Going through this book will be similar to what you would do in CBT sessions with me as your therapist. It will:

→ Help you explore your anger and underlying emotions

→ Show you ways to express your emotions in a healthy manner

→ Teach you how to advocate for yourself and communicate your needs in a respectful manner

→ Provide you with a variety of practical strategies and tools to manage your negative emotions, thoughts, and behaviors

→ Give you a safe space to write and reflect about your negative emotions and thoughts

→ Provide you with support and encouragement as you process difficult emotions

CBT is evidence based, meaning its techniques have been studied widely and have consistently proven results. It's a short-term therapy, meaning it could take anywhere from a few sessions to a few years to reach therapeutic goals. This differs from regular talk therapy, which could go on for a lifetime and usually encourages clients to rely on the therapist for ongoing emotional support. CBT clients aren't dependent on the therapist for ongoing support; instead, they learn to manage their emotions in sessions and then implement techniques outside the sessions. When it comes to anger management, relying exclusively on a weekly 45-minute therapy session to process and manage anger is not enough, because anger doesn't just happen once a week. You need to learn techniques that you can use whenever anger strikes.

Keep in mind that this book is a great way to understand, manage, and work through anger; however, ongoing aggressive behaviors or debilitating guilt, depression, trauma, other underlying mental health problems, or physical symptoms should be addressed by a mental health or medical professional. This book is not a replacement for medical or mental health treatment. There is no shame in seeking help from a professional; in fact, it takes courage to do so.

How to Use This Book to Reach Your Goals

YOU'RE ON THE PATH TOWARD CONTROLLING YOUR ANGER, and working through this book is an excellent step.

In order to get the most out of this workbook, it's best to work through the chapters in order. They're organized in a way that will help you be successful in improving your anger management using CBT techniques, and it's the same structure I use to treat anger problems in sessions. First, you'll learn all about anger. Then you'll learn about CBT and how it can treat unhealthy anger. Next, you'll have an opportunity to explore your anger patterns and triggers, after which you'll be prepared to learn ways to change your negative thoughts and behaviors using CBT techniques. You'll then receive tips on healthy communication and conflict resolution. After that, you'll learn about how to rebuild your relationships in a healthy way and about the importance of self-care (activities that are healthy for your mind and body). In the final chapter, you'll learn about ways to manage your anger long-term.

Each chapter has several components to help ensure your success. They provide you with emotional support as well as tools that will help you learn and retain the information. The chapters include affirmations to help motivate you on your journey. They include an "Anger Thermometer," a guided journaling section for you to process emotional triggers that may come up while going through the book. The relaxation tips help give you a break from your triggers and can be used to reduce anger-related tension when necessary. The anger-themed anecdotes and short stories will provide examples of how anger develops and different ways in which people express it. The reading sections and workbook exercises will help you learn and practice CBT anger management techniques. The chapter summaries and action items will help you retain and implement the information you learned.

This workbook contains 43 CBT exercises for anger management and 9 relaxation techniques. They're meant to help you change the way you think and act with regard to anger. I assure you that the exercises in this workbook have been designed to safely and gently help you start to manage your anger. They will allow you to reflect on and process your emotions, thoughts, and behaviors related to anger. They will increase your awareness of the consequences of unhealthy anger. They'll help you explore, identify, and process your "schemas," which are at the root of your anger. Schemas are your unique, deep underlying beliefs about yourself, others, the world, and the future. You'll also learn ways to challenge your negative schemas and come up with "balanced thoughts," which are factual statements that include positive and negative facts. And you'll gain some knowledge about relaxation techniques that will help you feel calmer and in control, rather than tense and easily angered. With ongoing practice, you'll be able to make positive changes in the way you (1) perceive situations that trigger your anger and (2) communicate your emotions, thoughts, and needs. These changes will help you ultimately take control over your anger.

The types of exercises in this workbook include: stress-reduction techniques (you'll find relaxation tips at the end of each chapter under the "Anger Thermometer" sections), thought pattern exploration (for example, see Understanding Your Schemas, page 38), cognitive restructuring (see Decatastrophizing and Finding Solutions, page 57), healthy communication strategies (see Healthy Boundaries, page 117), learning to respond instead of react to anger (see Preparatory Empathy, page 78), tips on healthy communication (see Using "I" Statements, page 92), and finding ways to improve your relationships (see Activity Scheduling for Loved Ones, page 116). The exercises are formatted as guided journaling entries, tracking logs, prompts with write-in lines, checklists, and fill-in tables. Some will require one day to complete and others will require several days.

Regardless of the time frames for the exercises, you should go through this book gradually and meticulously. Be sure to pay close attention to your emotions and be gentle with yourself. The content and exercises you'll find here are sensitive because they require you to think about your experiences with anger in as much detail as possible. This can become emotionally and mentally challenging, so taking your time will reduce your chances of feeling overwhelmed. In addition, focusing on one exercise at a time will give you the opportunity to really learn, implement, and reuse the techniques in your life. As you read through the sections, take notes, highlight important terminology and phrases, and use the affirmations that you relate to as daily mantras.

If you find yourself feeling negative emotions, consider the following: take breaks from the book, engage in healthy distractions, journal your thoughts and emotions in a separate diary and/or in the Anger Thermometer sections, or try out some relaxation techniques.

With the help of this book and with your thought, time, and hard work, you will be successful in managing your unhealthy anger.

UNDERSTANDING ANGER

Understanding my anger is the first step toward taking control over it. I am willing to do the hard work to achieve this goal.

This chapter includes the definition of anger, its origins, and how it can be healthy or unhealthy; a self-assessment illustrating the effect of anger on your life; what happens in the brain and body when people become angry; exercises to explore consequences of unhealthy anger and barriers to overcoming unhealthy anger; and a discussion of taking charge of your anger.

WHAT IS ANGER?

Anger is a powerful negative emotion that arises when people perceive a threat from an unexpected source and feel capable of taking action. When faced with threats, people naturally try to dissipate them by evading or fighting them. If they feel incapable of fighting the threat, they will usually experience vulnerable emotions such as fear, sadness, or embarrassment; this will usually result in avoiding or evading the threat. If they feel capable of fighting the threat, they will usually feel powerful emotions such as annoyance or anger; this will usually result in fighting the threat.

Anger is triggered by "perceived threats," which are threats that people believe to be real; however, just because a threat is perceived as real doesn't mean it actually is. "Actual threats" have real likelihoods of causing danger while "imagined threats" are only thought to do so. CBT techniques help with discerning between these threats.

When people feel angry, they perceive threats to their physical or emotional well-being. Physical threats are situations that jeopardize a person's physical safety, such as being assaulted or physically injured. Emotional threats are problems or stressors that threaten something that is important to a person, such as their integrity, respect from others, financial stability, or emotional security.

Anger can be communicated through: passive aggression, active aggression, or assertiveness. Passive aggression is hostile behavior that expresses negative emotions (such as resentment and anger) in an indirect and unclear manner. Active aggression is hostile behavior that directly expresses negative emotions and is emotionally, verbally, or physically threatening.

Anger can be healthy or unhealthy, depending on the type of threat and the way anger is communicated. Anger that is triggered by *actual* threats (not imagined) and expressed through assertiveness or active aggression (only to the point of dissipating the threats) can be healthy. Anger that is triggered by *imagined* threats and expressed by using healthy coping and communication techniques can also be healthy. Anger that is triggered by *imagined* threats and expressed through passive or active aggression is unhealthy.

Healthy anger involves assertiveness, relaxation techniques, self-care, and/or "cognitive restructuring" (changing the way a person perceives situations). Unhealthy anger involves passive aggression, unwarranted active aggression, "hyperarousal" (being on high alert), a lack of self-care, and/or ruminating about negative thoughts.

Unhealthy anger develops in many ways. When emotional threats are perceived as unresolvable, they may result in unhealthy anger. When people lack success with expressing or being in touch with vulnerable emotions, unhealthy anger may develop. Some people learned from their caregivers and peers that aggression is the best way to dissipate emotional threats. Some people develop unhealthy anger after experiencing maltreatment or other traumatic events. Sudden brain injuries can also cause unhealthy anger if one of the parts of the brain that controls decision-making or emotion regulation is affected. Certain health conditions, disabilities, and medications can lead to unhealthy anger as well. And lastly, some substances and physiological states can increase the likelihood of unhealthy anger.

Anger Can Be Healthy

Anger is one of the body's natural responses to feeling stressed or threatened. It springs people into action rather than letting them feel helpless. Without healthy anger, people would only avoid or run away from problems and never face them. Healthy anger can help people be assertive in expressing their needs, desires, and concerns. It can motivate them to succeed at something. It can help them protest social injustices. It can give them the courage to defend themselves or others in situations where actual threats exist.

In order to express anger in a healthy way, one must learn to *respond* to anger instead of *react*. Responding requires slowing down and thinking about the next steps, as well as the consequences. When people respond to their anger, they give themselves the chance to make better decisions about how to process and express it. Responding to anger allows people the space and time to practice assertiveness, relaxation techniques, self-care, healthy decision-making, and cognitive restructuring. By using these techniques, anger can become a healthy part of people's lives. Responding to anger might still result in some negative consequences, but the consequences are usually less severe than if the person would have reacted to it.

When Anger Becomes Unhealthy

When people *react* instead of *respond* to their anger, it becomes unhealthy. Reacting involves acting quickly and without thought or regard for the consequences. When the consequences aren't taken into consideration, anger is more likely to be misdirected and communicated aggressively; therefore, people may do or say things that are out of character (such as making hurtful comments, harming themselves or others, or damaging property).

Unhealthy anger can cause physiological, emotional, social, mental, financial, and legal issues. Physiologically, people experience muscle tension, which can lead to pain or discomfort. They may experience health issues as a result of ongoing anger issues. Emotionally, people may experience low self-esteem, depression, anxiety, irritability, hopelessness, guilt, or sadness. Some may spend so much time feeling angry that they don't enjoy their lives as much. Socially, individuals may experience estrangement from friends, which can eventually lead to loneliness. They may have conflicts with peers, coworkers, family members, or strangers. They might burn bridges, which can make it difficult to reconnect with others or be considered for employment opportunities. They may have difficulties concentrating, which can affect safety, work performance, academic abilities, and other responsibilities. People can lose jobs or fail academically, which can cause self-esteem and financial problems. Or they might encounter legal problems, which would likely cause additional emotional stress, lengthy and stressful court appearances, or even jail time.

Anger can also become a problem when it's not expressed at all, which is a different but also harmful way of reacting to the feeling of anger. Repressed anger takes up energy and physiological resources; it can lead to passive-aggressive behavior, physical health issues like diabetes and heart problems, and mental health issues like depression and anxiety.

EXERCISE: ANGER SELF-ASSESSMENT

Increase your awareness of the impact of unhealthy anger on your life. Circle the number that corresponds to your answer for each statement, tally up your score, and then look at the score interpretation at the bottom. Please note that this assessment and score interpretations are not substitutes for a clinical assessment and diagnosis from a health professional.

Quiz: How Much Does Anger Affect Your Life?

STATEMENT	NEVER	RARELY	SOMETIMES	OFTEN
I'm able to get past my moments of anger in a short period of time.	4	3	2	1
I get tense muscles and/or body aches.	1	2	3	4
I communicate well with others.	4	3	2	1
I have anger outbursts.	1	2	3	4
I respond, rather than react, to my anger.	4	3	2	1
I feel embarrassed as a result of my anger reactions.	1	2	3	4
I eat unhealthy foods or drinks after episodes of anger.	1	2	3	4
I sleep well, regardless of my anger.	4	3	2	1
I throw items during moments of anger.	1	2	3	4
I start arguments and/or fights.	1	2	3	4
I scare people with my anger reactions.	1	2	3	4
Before expressing my anger, I use healthy coping techniques to calm down.	4	3	2	1

People openly disagree with me without fear of getting yelled at.	4	3	2	1
I can put my anger aside to focus on other things that need to be attended to.	4	3	2	1

Score total _____

SCORE INTERPRETATION:

14 to 28: Your anger doesn't affect your life much, but there is always room for improvement.

29 to 43: Your anger issues affect your life sometimes. You would benefit from some support and anger management techniques.

44 to 56: Anger affects your life a great deal. There's a lot to learn about your anger triggers, as well as ways to regulate and communicate your emotions.

Take a moment to reflect on your score and what it tells you:

_____

_____

Jessie

Jessie is 39 years old and has suffered from unhealthy anger for most of his life. When he was 7 years old, he ran across the street and was hit by a motorcycle. He was in a coma for two months. He recovered from the coma and completed rehab to be able to walk again. Unfortunately, he was diagnosed with a traumatic brain injury.

When he returned home, he was different. Prior to the accident, he had a close relationship with his 6-year-old brother, Nolan. Now he found himself hitting and yelling at Nolan often. Nolan would cry, and their father would hit Jessie as a form of discipline. Jessie did well in school academically but was also starting fights with peers there. Eventually, when Jessie went through a growth spurt, he would fight his father back when he was disciplined, in order to defend himself. At age 13, Jessie's parents decided to send him to a boarding high school for teens with behavioral issues. They were hoping that there he would learn how to manage his aggression. While there, Jessie witnessed and got into several physical altercations with his peers. His aggression only worsened. And so did his anger toward his family. He was angry at his father for abusing him, his mother for not protecting him, his brother for "being a crybaby" whenever Jessie hit him, and his family for "abandoning" him in a boarding school.

Jessie was angry at the world. He felt like the world owed him for all the pain he had gone through. He saw himself as a victim of life. The motorcyclist who hit him and his family members were all to blame for his problems. Because he lacked a sense of personal responsibility for his anger and actions, he couldn't keep a steady job. He thought that supervisors who knew about his brain injury should be understanding and lenient with him. He did not respect authority figures and had difficulties taking orders from managers, so he would often have anger outbursts whenever they asked him to get off his phone or get to work on time.

Jessie's brain injury caused issues with impulse control, which led to reacting to his anger using active aggression. As a result of Jessie's physical safety being threatened (from being hit by the motorcycle, being abused by his father, and witnessing the fights at school), his perception of others and the world became tainted. He developed schemas such as "People are dangerous and cruel," "No one cares about me," and "People want to hurt me." He lived in a persistently negative emotional state, constantly experienced hyperarousal, perceived people as threatening, and often felt like he needed to defend himself. In order to manage his anger, Jessie would need to change his schemas and learn and implement healthy coping techniques to help him respond to his anger instead of react.

MIND, BODY, AND ANGER

When people feel angry, it's usually because of a perceived threat. The body has a system that helps people survive threats, and it's called the sympathetic nervous system ("SNS," also known as the "fight-or-flight" response). It prepares the body to deal with danger by causing changes throughout the body that allow humans (and many other animal species) to "fight" a threat or "flee" away from it. It was originally meant to help people survive physical threats such as the lack of food, shelter, or safety (and it does still get activated when people experience these threats). However, even with minimal physical threats to survival in developed countries, the SNS is continually activated in humans because of emotional threats. Threats cause the brain to send signals to the body to activate the SNS and prepare the brain and body to face or escape danger. In this state, humans are hyper focused on fighting or escaping threats, are more aware of their surroundings, produce more energy, suppress hunger, and are able to move quickly.

What's Happening in the Brain?

When faced with an emotional threat, the part of the brain called the amygdala activates the fight-or-flight response. The amygdala is two almond-shaped groups of cells at the base of the brain responsible for processing emotions, emotional behavior, and emotional memory. This part of the brain is sometimes referred to as the "emotional brain," and is primarily active during anger *reactions*. During anger *responses*, a different part of the brain is primarily active: the frontal lobes. The frontal lobes lie behind the forehead and are responsible for language and speech, emotional regulation, social behavior, personality, planning, decision-making, body movements, information processing, and self-awareness. When people are able to use assertiveness and rational thinking, it's because of this part of the brain; therefore, it is sometimes referred to as the "rational brain."

When the SNS is activated, people may either retreat from the threat (by getting away from the stressor and/or exhibiting vulnerable emotions) or attack the threat (by using passive or active aggression). When the amygdala is in control, the frontal lobes lack control, and people act on instinct and fear. They don't think about the consequences of their words or actions. Without the help of the frontal lobes, people can't assess situations clearly, nor can they communicate with assertiveness. This could easily result in intense anger or emotional outbursts.

What's Happening in the Body?

Once the brain recognizes a threat, it sends a signal to the body's adrenal glands. These glands produce the hormones epinephrine (also known as adrenaline) and norepinephrine. These hormones suppress appetite and the immune system so that the body can focus its energy on protecting itself from the threat. They increase heart rate and blood sugar levels in order to increase energy and strength. If the anger is intense, the body may produce high amounts of epinephrine. This may affect the senses by dilating the pupils (for brighter and broader vision), sharpening the sense of hearing, and reducing the ability to feel pain (in order to tolerate injuries). It can also cause hot flashes, sweating, skin flushing, headaches or migraines, high blood pressure, jitters, or hyperventilation.

When these hormones increase the heart rate, blood flows from the small muscle groups (including extremities and skin) to the large muscle groups (such as the limbs). This allows the large muscles to become tense and strong so that they can react more quickly. As a result of the reduced blood flow to the small muscles, hands and feet may become cold and skin may become pale with goose bumps.

When epinephrine and norepinephrine increase blood sugar (glucose) levels, the body creates more energy (for fighting or running away from threats) and blood thickens (to prepare for injury). Here's a brief explanation of how glucose interacts with the body when people experience unhealthy anger: Glucose enters the blood from the carbohydrates people ingest. A natural hormone called insulin allows the body's cells to be receptive to the glucose. After entering the cells, the glucose is converted to energy that the body will use right away. Since people don't need endless amounts of energy, not all the glucose is sent to the cells. Insulin turns the excess glucose into glycogen, which gets stored in the liver and/or muscles. As the body requires more energy to react to threats, epinephrine breaks down the stored glycogen into glucose. The glucose is transferred to the blood again so that insulin can convert it to energy. Repeatedly experiencing these glucose changes will eventually lead to serious health issues (this will be discussed in chapter 8).

In addition to the hormonal changes that happen during anger episodes, the body also makes changes that demonstrate negative emotions. Some examples include a clenched jaw, clenched fists, raised shoulders, crossed arms, furrowed brows, frowning, and wide darting eyes.

EXERCISE: CONSEQUENCES OF UNHEALTHY ANGER

This exercise will increase your awareness of the effects of unhealthy anger on your life. For the next seven days, log anything that annoys, frustrates, or angers you (the trigger).

DAY OF THE WEEK	TRIGGER	BEHAVIOR

Patterns:

_____

_____

_____

_____

Then log your behavior and the consequences, including physical symptoms, other emotions, and social issues. Do you notice any patterns? List them in the lines following the table.

PHYSICAL SYMPTOMS	OTHER EMOTIONS	SOCIAL CONSEQUENCES

Patterns:

_____

_____

_____

_____

_____

EXERCISE: HOW HAS UNHEALTHY ANGER HELPED YOU?

One of the reasons why people experience unhealthy anger repeatedly is that it has gotten them results. For example, it's possible that unhealthy anger has gotten you what you want because people listen to you when you yell. Read through this checklist and check off any statements that you can relate to. Then write down your own statements if you have more to add.

☐ People listen the best when I yell.

☐ People know I mean business when I raise my voice.

☐ People respect me because I'm tough with them.

☐ My aggression shows people that I won't be taken advantage of.

☐ If I'm not aggressive, I'll come off as weak.

☐ If I speak in a calm tone of voice when I'm angry, people won't understand how I really feel.

☐ I feel better after yelling at people.

☐ I feel better after acting passive aggressively toward people who annoy or anger me.

☐ My self-harming behavior dissipates my anger.

Now add your own:

_____

_____

_____

_____

TAKING CHARGE OF YOUR ANGER

Anger management isn't about learning to suppress your anger. Suppressing your anger will only worsen it and lead to other negative emotions and health issues. Anger can be a useful emotion when directed properly, so that's part of the goal here. When you manage your anger, you learn how to use it as motivation to advocate for positive causes and communicate assertively. You learn how to avoid using aggression to express your anger.

But what if unhealthy anger gets you results? What if it gets people to agree with or respect you? What if it gets people to understand how strongly you feel about something? What if it helps you regain a sense of power and control in situations where you feel taken advantage of? Even if aggression has helped you in some way, the negative consequences aren't worth it. The good news is that there are healthy alternative ways to achieve these goals. You can use assertiveness to communicate your needs and desires in a firm, direct, and respectful way. You can use a calm tone of voice to communicate your anger. You can regain your sense of power by controlling your emotions, changing your "automatic thoughts" (thoughts that come up immediately in response to situations), and changing the way you respond to your anger. You can distance yourself from the person or situation that's triggering your anger.

If you have pent-up aggression that needs to be released, researchers have found that it's best to use relaxation and cognitive behavioral techniques to calm your anger. On occasion, though, it's okay to let out some aggression using a safe outlet. You can do things like punch a mattress or scream into a pillow. Or you can engage in extracurricular activities that require physical energy, like working out, playing sports, or doing martial arts.

With the anger management CBT techniques in this workbook, you'll learn how to slow down your mind and body. You'll learn how to pause your *reactions* to anger so that you can *respond* instead. You'll practice using the frontal lobes of your brain rather than allowing the amygdala to take over. You'll explore and understand the underlying vulnerable emotions that are at the root of your anger. You'll become intimately familiar with your automatic thoughts, schemas, and common triggers that drive your anger so that you can take control over them.

With practice, you'll eventually get used to catching yourself whenever you feel strong negative emotions. You'll be able to make healthier assessments about where they originate from. You'll learn how to manage them in healthy ways. And you'll learn how to clearly and respectfully communicate your needs and wishes so that your anger is less likely to be triggered.

When you learn to manage your emotions and become a better communicator, you'll feel better. Your self-esteem will improve. You'll have the tools to resolve conflicts more easily. And you'll be able to strengthen your current relationships, as well as establish and maintain healthy new ones.

EXERCISE: ANGER DIARY

Increasing your awareness of your anger triggers, negative thoughts, and the consequences of your anger reactions can be helpful so that you can take control over them. Get yourself a diary that's specifically for writing about anger situations, and try to log daily. Then you can take some of the situations you logged and apply them to the exercises in this workbook. If you aren't able to get a diary just yet, start in the lines provided.

_____

_____

_____

_____

_____

_____

_____

_____

_____

Anger Thermometer

Take a moment for self-care. Are you having any emotional triggers based on the topics discussed in this chapter? Any thoughts related to anger, passive aggression, or active aggression? Any triggers related to the impact of unhealthy anger on your life, such as health issues, problems with daily functioning, or social or legal troubles? Any triggers related to where your anger might have originated? Did the story bring up any triggers related to physical abuse, abandonment, or traumatic brain injury?

Write about any triggers here, and if necessary, try the relaxation tip below.

_____

_____

_____

_____

_____

_____

_____

_____

_____

_____

_____

Relaxation Tip: Body Scan and Self-Massage

If you're feeling any tension or body aches, you might benefit from a relaxation technique. Take a moment to analyze where your body tension is. Start with a body scan. Imagine scanning your body from head to toe for any tension. Give attention to your:

Forehead	*Shoulders*	*Thighs*
Eyes	*Chest*	*Calves*
Ears	*Abdomen*	*Feet*
Jaw	*Arms*	*Toes*
Neck	*Hands*	

Then, attending to one part at a time, try massaging that part of your body until it feels relaxed or less painful. Engaging in self-massage is one of many techniques that can help with controlling your anger. When you manage your physiological reactions to anger, it slows down the fight-or-flight response so that you can respond to anger.

CHAPTER TAKEAWAYS

→ Anger is a powerful negative emotion that arises when people perceive a threat from an unexpected source and feel capable of taking action. It is a natural emotion that can be managed in healthy ways and directed toward healthy causes. Anger can be communicated with passive aggression, active aggression, or assertiveness.

→ Anger is triggered by "perceived threats," which can be actual or imagined. CBT techniques help with discerning actual from imagined threats.

→ Anger affects the way the brain works. It causes physiological changes and discomforts. It has social and personal consequences.

→ Unhealthy anger may get results, but the consequences are not worth it. There are healthy ways to express anger. There are better ways to let out pent-up aggression.

→ The amygdala makes up the "emotional brain" while the frontal lobes make up the "rational brain." When people *react* to anger, it's because the emotional brain is primarily activated. When they *respond* to anger, it's because the rational brain is primarily activated.

TAKE IT FORWARD

→   Try to be more aware of your body's reactions to anger. Notice moments when you're not facing actual threats, but your body is telling you that you are.

→   Try becoming aware of what is being threatened when you become angry. Is your integrity being threatened? Your sense of emotional security? Your relationships? Try to notice patterns and write them down in your anger management diary.

→   In general, try keeping a calm demeanor. If your baseline mood and demeanor are calm, then it will be more difficult to become angry. Keep a calm tone of voice. Speak slowly, breathe deeply through your nose, and have a neutral posture. Keep your face and body as relaxed as possible.

Anger and aggression don't have to go hand in hand. Anger-driven aggression will not define me. I will take control over my aggression by managing my physiological reactions.

2

CBT FOR ANGER MANAGEMENT

I will have a solution-focused mentality so that I
experience fewer emotional threats.
I will learn to resolve my issues without
anger-driven aggression.

This chapter explains cognitive behavior therapy and
describes a CBT session. It explains what makes CBT techniques so helpful for anger management, and offers some
exercises that will help you practice exploring automatic
thoughts and schemas.

CBT EXPLAINED

Cognitive behavior therapy is based on the notion that thoughts, feelings, and behaviors all affect each other but are separate from one another. If a person can change the way they think, then they can change the way they act. If they can change the way they feel emotionally and physically, this can help them change the way they behave. If a person can change the way they behave, then they can change the way they feel and think. When people feel angry and *react* to it, it's because the associated thoughts are focused on helplessness. If they feel angry and *respond* to it, then the associated thoughts are solution-focused. If people can change the way they look at stressors— mainly by looking at them as problems that can be solved—then their anger can yield positive results.

CBT encourages people to look at their automatic thoughts (which everyone has) in different situations so that they can be changed if necessary. Automatic thoughts can be positive or negative, and they typically lead to the emotions people experience. People have no control over the initiation of these thoughts and beliefs, but they can make decisions on what to do with them. They can choose to *react* to them, or they can choose to change them and *respond* differently.

In order to change a person's thoughts, they would need to first slow down. After slowing down, people can use the rational brain (frontal lobes), rather than primarily the emotional brain (amygdala). With the rational brain, they can analyze perceived threats, their automatic thoughts, their schemas (beliefs people have about themselves, others, the world, and the future), the facts of the situation, the actions they want to take, and the consequences they might face. Processing this information allows people to make informed decisions about their anger, so that they're less likely to face negative consequences. It also allows them the opportunity to change the way they feel about and view the situation.

Evidence Based

Many studies have proven that CBT is effective in treating several issues and disorders, so this categorizes it as evidence based. Research on CBT as a treatment for anger and aggression has focused on various age groups, including adults, adolescents, and children; combat veterans; people who have been convicted of violent offenses; athletes with aggression problems; and people with coexisting cognitive issues, such as intellectual disabilities, learning disabilities, traumatic brain injury, ADHD, and high-functioning autism. Studies have also included individuals with emotional issues like depression, anxiety, and posttraumatic stress disorder (PTSD).

Goal Oriented

CBT can be used in individual therapy or in programs targeted for specific populations, but regardless it's goal oriented. In individual therapy, the goals and components depend on the client's needs and progress. In a program, the goals and components are typically predetermined. In both individual CBT and CBT programs, the goals are discussed at the start of treatment and are addressed during every session to help clients and clinicians stay focused on the goals, as well as to track progress. The goals for anger management CBT (and this workbook) are to:

→ Separate emotions, thoughts, and behaviors

→ Identify automatic thoughts and schemas

→ Challenge negative schemas

→ Develop alternative ways of thinking by building empathy toward the people who trigger one's anger

→ Increase assertiveness and solution-focused thinking

→ Reduce aggressive behavior

Time Limited

Along with being goal oriented, CBT is time limited, meaning it's a short-term therapy that can take anywhere from a few sessions to a few years. This is because CBT teaches skills that clients can use between sessions and beyond. Eventually, clients won't need the weekly sessions to manage their anger. Once a client is able to consistently practice healthy coping skills outside of sessions, the therapeutic goals have been met and therapy can end.

Going through this workbook will also be time limited, because there is a set number of exercises to complete and you'll probably get through the book within a few weeks to a few months.

Regular psychotherapy, on the other hand, is not time limited. The goal in this type of therapy is to undo the emotional damage experienced by clients throughout their lifetimes. The therapist provides emotional support during weekly sessions to help clients internalize love and acceptance. As you can imagine, this deep healing process takes time.

Past Affects Present

CBT is mostly focused on the here and now, but past experiences are important to explore because they affect the way people currently see themselves, others, and the future. Individuals' schemas are developed as a result of childhood and other significant experiences. When I conduct CBT sessions, we explore relevant past experiences to help clients understand their current schemas. Negative schemas are often based on one or more adverse experiences from the past, and they're usually not applicable to current experiences. The way people perceive situations is not always an accurate account of what actually happened. So, in the sessions, I help clients recognize the ways in which their schemas affect their perception of current experiences.

Active Participation

CBT works best when the client takes on an active role in their own anger management journey. For instance, one technique called "cognitive restructuring" involves the client identifying and changing their irrational automatic thoughts. In a session, the client discusses a specific situation involving strong emotions, as well as the related automatic thoughts. Then the client is prompted with questions to help them explore, identify, and analyze their deep underlying beliefs (schemas). They're asked to identify evidence for and against the schemas. This allows clients to give themselves a reality check. As mentioned before, unhealthy anger is processed by the emotional brain (amygdala). By going through this reality check, it allows the rational brain (frontal lobes) to discover balanced thoughts. The balanced thoughts will then replace any irrational beliefs, and this results in more rational behavior.

EXERCISE: EXPLORING AUTOMATIC THOUGHTS

Automatic thoughts come up, well, automatically, and they determine our emotions, so it's important to have some practice with identifying them. Notes on automatic thoughts:

→ They are statements, not questions.

→ They can be assumptions or facts.

→ They can be schemas or just temporary thoughts about a specific situation.

In the first half of this exercise, literally draw a line to match the situation to the automatic thought. There are no right or wrong answers. The point of the first half of the exercise is to familiarize yourself with situations and automatic thoughts that could surface as a result.

In the second half, list your own anger-triggering situations and automatic thoughts.

SITUATION	AUTOMATIC THOUGHT
My partner hasn't responded to my last message, which was three hours ago, but has been posting content on social media since then.	They don't value me.
My best friend surprised me on my lunch break to go eat at my favorite restaurant.	They're ignoring me.
My parents didn't call me on my birthday, but they call me all the time for money.	They care about me.
My boss offered me a title change without a raise.	They're using me.

Now list your own anger-triggering situations and automatic thoughts:

Situation: _____

Automatic thoughts: _____

_____

_____

Situation: _____

Automatic thoughts: _____

_____

_____

_____

Situation: _____

Automatic thoughts: _____

_____

_____

Situation: _____

Automatic thoughts: _____

_____

_____

Cheryl

Cheryl, now in her 50s, was diagnosed with an intellectual disability and hyperthyroidism (a disorder that can cause fatigue) as a child. Her mother felt ashamed of her because of her cognitive difficulties. She would make abusive comments to Cheryl and would "jokingly" tell people that her daughter was "slow." Cheryl was able to complete high school but lacked the confidence and resources to succeed in college.

At age 18, Cheryl became pregnant and told her partner about it. A young man himself, he wasn't ready for a relationship or to be a father. So, he disappeared from her life. She raised her son, Charles, alone, with financial help from the government. She loved her son more than anything in the world, but she often felt lonely, down on herself, and depressed. As soon as Charles learned some empathy and independence (around age three), Cheryl would go to him for emotional support.

Because she was unemployed, her sister would ask for help with watching her son who was close in age to Charles. While babysitting, Cheryl often became angry. She would yell at her son and nephew for any misbehavior or for making mistakes. When she felt overwhelmed with anger, she would sob in anguish while pulling chunks of her hair out in front of them. One time, she yelled at her 8-year-old nephew, kicked him out of her apartment, and slammed the door in his face, leaving him scared and alone in the hallway. As her son and nephew grew older, they kept their distance from her as much as possible to avoid dealing with her anger-driven aggression.

At age 35, Cheryl met someone and shortly after they were married. Unfortunately, her partner was emotionally abusive toward her. They would name-call her and didn't allow her to leave the house because they were possessive. She gave the marriage a chance for one year but ended up divorcing them.

More recently, she's been less actively aggressive, but her anger remains a problem. When people don't prioritize her needs, she feels unloved. Feeling unloved reminds her of the lack of love from her mother, son's father, and ex-spouse. This makes her feel badly about herself and helpless about it, and then angry as a result. When she's angry now, she becomes tense but remains quiet, and it's obvious that something is wrong. This makes people uncomfortable during family gatherings.

Cheryl previously expressed her anger through active aggression, but now she uses passive aggression. Both types of aggression have caused issues in her life and relationships. Her negative schemas have caused her to experience unhealthy anger. They include "I'm stupid," "I'm unworthy of love," "People are cruel," and "Life is horrible." These schemas cause her to have negative automatic thoughts and an overly negative outlook on life.

EXERCISE: BALANCED THOUGHTS
MIX AND MATCH

When you become angry, you're typically focusing on only your negative beliefs, whether or not there's evidence to support them (dialectical thinking will be covered later in chapter 4). Once you examine the evidence and identify the facts, you can explore more balanced thoughts. Try this exercise to help you become familiar with and practice putting together balanced beliefs. This practice will be helpful for when you start using "CBT Thought Records" (page 154–157). Draw lines to connect a statement from the "Evidence for" column to the matching "Evidence against" column. The exercise is headed with a schema for context. Each "Evidence for" statement starts with the word "although," because this is the method I use when teaching my clients to complete the "Balanced Thoughts" column in CBT thought records. There are no right or wrong answers. The point of this exercise is to familiarize yourself with the format of balanced thoughts.

SCHEMA: I MAKE BAD DECISIONS.

EVIDENCE FOR	EVIDENCE AGAINST
Although I chose a hairdresser who messed up my haircut,	I got a good education that prepared me for my career.
Although I owe too much in student loans,	I've made the choice to learn from each experience and not repeat my mistakes.
Although I've chosen partners who aren't compatible with me,	Accepting this job was the best choice for me at the time.
Although I hate my current job,	They've always done a good job and this is the only time they have messed up my hair.

EXERCISE: BALANCED THOUGHTS

In the first part of this exercise, you'll fill in two balanced beliefs based on the schema listed. In the second part of this exercise, you'll add your own schema and balanced thoughts.

Note that balanced thoughts:

→ Are not based on opinions

→ Are factual statements that include both positive and negative aspects of situations

→ Include information about the past and present, not the future

→ Should contain information about the whole picture

Schema: "People can't be trusted."

Although I've been lied to in the past, _____.

Although some people have stolen from me, _____.

Now add your own schema:

_____

And balanced thoughts:

Although _____, _____.

Although _____, _____.

Anger Thermometer

Take a moment for self-care. Are you having any emotional triggers based on the topics discussed in this chapter? How did it feel to explore your automatic thoughts? Any struggles with coming up with balanced thoughts? Did Cheryl's story bring up any triggers for you? Did any of the examples in the exercises trigger negative emotions?

Write about any triggers here, and if necessary, try the relaxation tip below.

_____

_____

_____

_____

_____

_____

_____

_____

_____

_____

_____

_____

_____

_____

Relaxation Tip: Paced Breathing

Paced breathing, also known as "diaphragmatic breathing" or "slow controlled breathing," is a relaxation technique proven to decrease negative moods and reduce cortisol (stress hormone) levels. Try this out whenever you're experiencing anger or stress.

1. Start with a seated, relaxed body position. Be sure to have good posture so that you can get the most air into your lungs.

2. Close your eyes.

3. Take a slow deep breath in through your nose (or mouth if you can't breathe through your nose) as you feel your abdomen expanding. Your abdomen should expand while you inhale because your diaphragm (the large breathing muscle underneath your lungs) should be pulling down into the abdomen. This allows your lungs to expand so that they can take in more air.

4. As slowly as possible, exhale through your mouth while contracting your abdomen.

5. Repeat at least 10 times. This exercise should take a few minutes to complete.

CHAPTER TAKEAWAYS

→ Cognitive behavior therapy is based on the notion that thoughts, feelings, and behaviors all affect each other but are separate from one another. If a person can change the way they think, then they can change the way they feel and behave.

→ In order to change negative thinking patterns, you must learn to identify your automatic thoughts and schemas, question whether or not they are rational, explore the facts, and conclude with balanced thoughts.

→ When your thoughts are solution focused, you're more likely to express your anger in a healthy way. If you hold on to helpless thoughts or beliefs, then your anger is likely to be unhealthy.

→ CBT requires active participation. This entails bringing up situations that trigger strong negative emotions, identifying emotions and automatic thoughts, analyzing the evidence, and coming up with balanced thoughts.

→ By frequently discussing and journaling about emotions, automatic thoughts, and schemas, you'll be able to discover your patterns. Knowing your patterns increases your awareness so that you can be more likely to notice and challenge negative schemas when they are triggered.

TAKE IT FORWARD

→ Practice slowing down your thoughts, decisions, and actions by ending your evenings with paced breathing. You may not be able to control situations that trigger your anger, but you can take control over your physiological reactions to anger.

→ Because anger management goals are important to stay focused and keep track of progress, make a list of detailed goals for managing your anger. Use the following questions to define your specific goals and write down your answers in your anger diary.

→ Once I've achieved my goals, what would my behavior or demeanor be like?

→ What would my mood be like?

→ What would my relationships be like?

→ What would my interactions with others be like?

→ What would my lifestyle be like?

→ What would my health be like?

→ Set reminders to spend time on this workbook at least once a week. This will help you be consistent with applying the anger management techniques in your life.

→ During or after anger-triggering situations, try to identify and write down your automatic thoughts that came up.

I will learn to identify my automatic thoughts so that I can manage them. I will be able to change the way I feel and act during stressful situations.

3

ROOTS OF
YOUR ANGER

My adverse life experiences don't have to define me. I will become familiar with the triggers that make me feel unsafe so that I can be ready to manage my negative emotions.

This chapter will dive into the origins of your anger, automatic thoughts, and negative schemas. It will explore triggers in general and yours specifically, how they relate to negative schemas, and how your brain works with regard to them. You'll have the opportunity to complete several exercises that help you identify and uncover the roots of your automatic thoughts, negative schemas, and anger triggers.

WHAT'S CAUSING YOUR ANGER?

Uncovering the sources of your anger is an important first step. Identifying the real source of frustration or stress will help you communicate your emotions better and deal with them in a healthier, more constructive way. People can gain some insight into their sources of anger by looking at their traumatic past experiences.

Emotional Trauma

Emotional trauma is defined as the emotional impact of a deeply distressing experience in which a person faces an emotional or physical threat. Trauma can result from directly experiencing, witnessing, or being exposed to an event or events where one's physical safety or that of others is threatened. This "big T" trauma falls under the diagnosis of PTSD (posttraumatic stress disorder). Many of the symptoms of this disorder are related to anger. They include irritability, negative beliefs or expectations of oneself and the future, body tension, constant negative emotional state (like always being angry or anxious), anger outbursts, sleep difficulties, and inability to feel positive emotions.

Trauma can also result from one or more mild to moderate experiences wherein one's emotional safety is at risk. Examples include being lied to or bullied, feeling rejected, disappointing oneself or others, or experiencing emotional abuse. These "little t" traumas tend to lead to problems like depression, anxiety, and anger.

Traumatic experiences leave imprints in the brain. The brain has the capacity to make associations between experiences, emotions, and physiological reactions. So, when people experience stress from traumas, their brains and bodies remember the experiences so that they can quickly recognize similar experiences as threats in the future. This is the brain's way of protecting people from getting hurt again. When a person goes through something traumatic, their minds develop schemas. These schemas cause automatic thoughts that are unique to each trigger or situation.

Here's an anecdote to explain further. Harry, now 44 years old, has a partner, James. Harry and his older brothers were raised by their father. When Harry was a child, he was bullied by his older brothers and peers at school because he wasn't the best at sports. When Harry would tell his father about the bullying, Harry would be told to "toughen up." These emotionally traumatic experiences led to the development of the schemas "I can't do anything right," "People aren't supportive," and "People want to hurt my feelings." Eventually, Harry did "toughen up." He started fighting his brothers and the bullies at school whenever they teased him. Since then, he feels triggered and gets combative whenever his schemas are activated, which happens whenever he struggles with accomplishing a task. In his current relationship, when James tries to help Harry do something difficult, Harry feels triggered and snaps at James. Harry's automatic thoughts combine his schemas with this specific situation. His thoughts are "James thinks I'm dumb," "James is laughing at me," and "James thinks he's better than me."

Brain Trauma and Physiological Problems

Another source of unhealthy anger is brain trauma. An injury to the head that affects the brain is called "traumatic brain injury" (TBI). Injuries can range from mild to severe, and aggression and PTSD symptoms commonly co-occur with TBI. Specifically, if the frontal lobes are harmed, it may result in frequent anger and aggression because the rational brain cannot work well to regulate thoughts and emotions. Instead, the amygdala functions mostly on its own.

Just as trauma to the brain can result in unhealthy anger, other physiological problems and states can do the same. Fatigue and any related medical issues can result in unhealthy anger because the rational brain can't function well without adequate energy. When people are tired, the emotional brain takes over. The same happens when people feel hungry; they become predisposed to anger because they don't have adequate energy and their bodies think they're in starvation mode, and this is perceived as a threat to survival.

EXERCISE: UNDERSTANDING YOUR SCHEMAS

Adverse life experiences shape your schemas and can contribute to unhealthy anger. Reflect on some of your adverse experiences, and write about them here. If something is too difficult to write about, consider seeing a mental health professional to help you process it in a safe and confidential space. In this exercise, the amount of detail you include is up to you.

_____

_____

_____

_____

EXERCISE: GETTING TO SCHEMAS
FROM AUTOMATIC THOUGHTS

Explore your deep underlying beliefs and assumptions about yourself, the world, others, and the future. Become familiar with exploring schemas by reading through the following example. Then try to come up with schemas in the following write-in lines.
   Notes about schemas:

→   In order to identify a schema from an automatic thought, use the "downward arrow technique."

   →   Start with an automatic thought.

   →   Ask yourself this: If the [automatic thought] is true, then what does this say about me, the world, others, or the future?

   →   Keep asking yourself this question until you conclude with a statement that can be applicable to several other situations that trigger strong emotions in your life.

→ Note that a schema is not action oriented. The schema will look like one of these:

> → "I am/am not/can't_____."

> → "People are/aren't_____."

> → "The world/universe is _____."

> → "_____ will happen."

Example:

Situation: I failed my driver's exam again.

Emotions: anger, confusion, worry

Automatic thought: "I keep failing my driver's exam." Because this in itself doesn't apply to many other situations that trigger strong emotions, you'll ask yourself the schema exploring question: "If I keep failing my driver's exam, then what does this say about me, the world, others, or the future?"

↓

Answer (about the future): "I'm never going to get my driver's license."

↓

What schema is behind this belief about the future?

↓

Answer: *I'm a failure.*

This statement can be applied to other areas in a person's life; therefore, this would be the schema.

For the following exercises, assume the related emotion is anger. Keep asking yourself the schema-exploring question until you get to the deep underlying belief. Use the downward arrow technique in your anger diary to discover the schema.

Automatic thought: "My friend hasn't paid me back the money I lent them."

Schema: _____

Automatic thought: "I don't understand this new computer system we're using at work."

Schema: _____

Automatic thought: "I gave my partner everything and they still broke up with me."

Schema: _____

Possible answers:

→ *People can't be trusted.*

→ *I'm never going to be successful in life.*

→ *I can never be loved.*

Shelly

Shelly, now 45 years old, grew up with strict, abusive parents. At age 7, whenever she didn't get a perfect score on an assignment, her parents would make her kneel down on the pavement in their backyard to reread all the material covered in the homework. Then they would quiz her on the questions, and for every incorrect answer, they would hit her with a sandal. At age 9, Shelly started bed-wetting. Her parents would beat her whenever they discovered the accidents. Shelly learned that mistakes and less-than perfect performances were unacceptable and should therefore be punished.

As an adult, she became grateful to her parents for the motivation and work ethic they instilled into her. She didn't consider their parenting style to be abusive. Instead, she felt that they did what any good parent would do to raise their child to be successful. She is now the owner and CEO of a fashion company, but is a perfectionist and suffers from anxiety.

Shelly's anxiety causes difficulties with concentrating, so she has issues with time management and attention to detail. Whenever she makes a mistake and people notice it, she becomes angry and blames it on her employees. As a result, Shelly's company has a high turnover rate. This doesn't bother her because it's a prominent company and has a waiting list of potential employees. And she doesn't feel bad for the people she treats poorly because she feels she's toughening them up so that they can be successful like her.

Shelly struggles with self-acceptance and self-love. When she's alone and reflects on her mistakes, she lets her anger out on herself. She berates herself with words and sometimes aggressively yanks on her hair as a form of punishment. She avoids romantic relationships because she's too afraid of failure as a partner.

Shelly's anger originated from the abuse from her parents, but she is not ready to accept that. She would feel too guilty if she were to direct her anger toward them. To protect herself from feeling immense guilt, she directs her anger toward herself. In order to get past this anger, she would first have to be honest with herself about her anger toward her parents. She would have to learn new positive schemas (e.g., "I can make mistakes and still be a smart person.") by using cognitive restructuring. And she would have to work on reducing her anxiety through the use of CBT techniques like relaxation training and activity scheduling.

ANGER TRIGGERS AND THE SCHEMAS AND AUTOMATIC THOUGHTS BEHIND THEM

Anger triggers are events, people, places, and things that cause anger to surface. Anger triggers happen when people have experiences that remind them of their negative schemas, worry that the problem isn't going to get resolved, and want or need to do something about it. For example, if someone's negative schema is "I'm dumb," then whenever they make mistakes or struggle to complete tasks, it might trigger an anger reaction.

People make mistakes and struggle with tasks all the time, but they don't always feel angry. The difference lies in the automatic thoughts, which stem from schemas but are unique based on isolated situations. If someone's schema is "I'm smart and capable of figuring things out," their automatic thought may be "I can complete this challenging task." If this is the case, then their fight-or-flight response would not be triggered by making a mistake. Challenging activities would not be perceived as threats; instead, they would be perceived as opportunities to overcome adversity and to be proud of after success. When people know what situations do cause them emotional stress (triggers), they can work backward to decipher the automatic thoughts and, even deeper, the schemas that are responsible for the stress. By understanding the situation, they are better prepared to handle the trigger by asking for help ahead of time, engaging in some relaxation exercises, or challenging their negative schemas.

Sometimes it is people, not situations, that trigger anger. The anger can damage relationships. Here's an anecdote: Lisa, age 28, often feels annoyed and easily angered around her parents because of bad childhood experiences with them. As a child, Lisa was physically abused by her parents because they didn't know any other way to discipline her. They themselves were disciplined through corporal punishment as children so they believed they were being good, caring parents. As a result, Lisa has schemas about them such as "They don't love me," "They don't respect me," "They're impatient," and "They're abusive and controlling." Lisa now has children and brings them to visit her parents. She doesn't want the past to get in the way of having a healthy relationship with them now. But whenever she talks to her parents about her own parenting and they offer her unsolicited advice, she feels angry. And whenever they try to offer her children gifts or snacks without asking for her permission first, she also feels angry. She feels angry because her schemas from the past and their current behavior (triggers) combined make her feel disrespected by them. Her automatic thoughts in these situations are "They think they know better" and "They think I'm a bad parent."

EXERCISE: EXPLORING YOUR FEARS

Below are some emotional threats that could trigger anger. After each prompt, add a situation you experienced that resulted in anger and that was triggered by the emotional threat listed. If you can't think of a situation, write in an example of any situation that could be triggered by the emotional threat.

Fear of losing love:

_____

Fear of losing my integrity:

_____

Fear of losing my financial stability:

_____

Fear of losing my health:

_____

Fear of losing my safety:

_____

Fear of losing my time:

_____

EXERCISE: EXPLORING YOUR TRIGGERS

Reflect on the moments that you get angry most often. What are the places, people, circumstances, climates, and physiological states in which or with whom you find yourself becoming angry often? Complete the write-in lines below along with any patterns you notice. Are there any patterns?

Places:

_____

_____

_____

People:

_____

_____

_____

Circumstances (e.g., wasting time, being in crowds):

_____

_____

_____

Climates (e.g., hot, cloudy):

_____

_____

_____

Physiological states (e.g., cold, sick, in pain, tired, hungry):

_____

_____

Other:

_____

_____

Anger Thermometer

Take a moment for self-care. Are you having any emotional triggers based on the content of this chapter? Any thoughts related to emotional or physical trauma? Any thoughts about your own physical health or energy? Did the stories bring up any triggers for you? Any triggers related to abuse, self-harm, perfectionism, low self-esteem, or self-directed anger? Did any of the examples in the exercises trigger negative emotions?

Write about any triggers here, and if necessary, try the relaxation tip on page 46.

_____

_____

_____

_____

_____

→

Relaxation Tip: Left Nostril Breathing

Studies have shown that breathing through the left nostril for a short period of time can help reduce sympathetic nervous system (SNS) activity. The SNS is the system that is activated during the fight-or-flight response. Left nostril breathing can also reduce your blood pressure and heart rate. Reducing the SNS's activity means the amygdala is not working as hard. This means your frontal lobes can chime in to help you think rationally about anger-triggering situations. Try this deep-breathing technique, using the left nostril only.

1. Start in a seated, relaxed, upright position.

2. With your right hand, palms open and facing your left side, take your right thumb and close your right nostril.

3. Inhale for 5 seconds.

4. Exhale for 5 seconds.

5. Repeat the cycle 10 times.

CHAPTER TAKEAWAYS

→ Anger triggers are events, people, places, and circumstances that cause anger to surface.

→ Traumatic experiences leave imprints in the brain. The brain has the capacity to make associations between experiences, emotions, and physiological reactions. So, when people experience stress from traumas, their brains and bodies remember the experiences so that they can quickly recognize similar experiences as threats in the future.

→ "Big T" trauma refers to the impact from directly experiencing, witnessing, or being exposed to an event or events where your physical safety or that of others is threatened. "Little t" traumas are experiences in which your emotional safety is threatened.

→ Schemas can help explain your triggers. If your schemas are negative, then you're more likely to perceive situations negatively. If your schemas are positive, then you're more likely to perceive them positively.

→ Unhealthy anger can surface through fatigue or hunger because the rational brain can't function well without adequate energy.

TAKE IT FORWARD

→ When you will be in or around triggering situations or people, try some relaxation techniques prior to or during, in order to reduce the chances of unhealthy anger.

→ As you go about your week, try to bring awareness to the connections between your anger triggers and your schemas.

→ Try to think about your schemas some more. The more aware you are of them, the better you'll get at identifying and challenging their resultant negative irrational thoughts that trigger anger.

→ Because hunger and fatigue can make it more likely for you to feel angry, aim to eat three healthy meals per day, with whole-food snacks (like fruits, vegetables, or nuts) in between. And make it a point to get enough rest (for adults, it's usually seven to nine hours a night), drink plenty of water, and address any medical issues with a medical professional.

I deserve to have a more positive outlook on the world.
I deserve to feel relaxed and safe in my daily experiences.
I deserve to be viewed as a respectful person by the people around me.

4

THINKING
DIFFERENTLY

*I will be honest with myself and
others about my emotions so that
I can address them.*

This chapter focuses on cognitive distortions—like polarized thinking, blaming, and catastrophizing—what they are, and how they relate to negative automatic thoughts and schemas. It then goes on to discuss ways to combat distortions, such as through decatastrophizing, dialectical thinking, exploring balanced thoughts, relaxation techniques, and mindfulness. Exercises center on identifying these distortions and working to replace them with balanced thinking.

UNDERSTANDING NEGATIVE THINKING

When people have irrational schemas and automatic thoughts, it's because of the cognitive distortions that exist in their minds. Cognitive distortions are distorted ways of thinking that were developed unconsciously as a result of adverse experiences. They contribute to negative schemas and negative automatic thoughts, which then contribute to strong negative emotions like anger. Once a person is able to recognize cognitive distortions in their automatic thoughts and schemas, they'll be able to recognize irrational thought patterns more easily. Recognizing these negative patterns will help with challenging them, which will in turn reduce unhealthy anger. Here are some of the common cognitive distortions.

Polarized thinking: Also known as "black-and-white thinking" or "all-or-nothing thinking," it is thinking in extremes, or feeling that individuals or situations are either all good or all bad.

Example: You believe your child always disrespects you because they sometimes don't do as they're told.

Jumping to conclusions: Making negative conclusions based on little information. You can do this through "mind reading" (believing you know someone's thoughts without explicitly hearing them say the words) or "fortune telling" (predicting that something negative will happen in the future).

Example: Your friend keeps saying they're too busy to hang out so you conclude that they're upset at you about something.

Catastrophizing: Also known as "catastrophic thinking," it means believing the worst-case scenario will happen.

Example: You made a small mistake at work and now you believe you will be fired.

Blaming: Holding others responsible for your feelings and behaviors.

Example: Your partner spends time with their friends without you sometimes, and you don't have many friends to spend time with. You blame your partner for your loneliness.

Filtering out the positive: Also known as "mental filtering," it means only focusing on the negative.

Example: Your parent visited you in the hospital five out of the six days you were there, and you feel angry because they missed one day.

Should statements: Believing things "should" be a certain way.

Example: Getting angry because your coworker got a promotion, but it should have been you.

Personalization: Taking things personally, even if they don't have anything to do with you.

Example: Your partner is stressed out about a family issue and has been distant. You're angry because you assume that the reason for their distance is that they're upset at you about something.

Emotional reasoning: Identifying a person's own feelings about a situation as evidence for their negative automatic thoughts.

Example: You feel embarrassed in a situation, so this must mean that others are laughing at you, and this leads to anger.

EXERCISE: POLARIZED THINKING

This cognitive distortion often uses absolute language, such as:

→ Always/never

→ Only/just

→ Every/all/none

→ Must/has to

Reflect on some anger-triggering situations. Did you have any "all-or-nothing" thoughts? Complete the following section to help increase your awareness of this cognitive distortion and come up with more balanced ways of thinking.

Here's an example:

All-or-nothing thought: *People are always rude to me.*

Balanced thought: *Although people are rude sometimes, sometimes they're nice to me.*

All-or-nothing thought:

_____

Balanced thought:

_____

All-or-nothing thought:

_____

Balanced thought:

_____

All-or-nothing thought:

_____

Balanced thought:

_____

All-or-nothing thought:

_____

Balanced thought:

_____

All-or-nothing thought:

_____

Balanced thought:

_____

EXERCISE: JUMPING TO CONCLUSIONS

Practice recognizing when you're jumping to conclusions, including through mind reading or fortune-telling. Complete the following prompts using any situations that triggered your anger.

Situation that angered me:

_____

_____

Conclusions I jumped to:

_____

_____

Situation that angered me:

_____

_____

Conclusions I jumped to:

_____

_____

Situation that angered me:

_____

_____

Conclusions I jumped to:

_____

_____

EXERCISE: EXPLORING THE EVIDENCE

In order to challenge negative schemas, people must explore the evidence (facts) that proves the schemas to be true, as well as evidence that shows them to be false. Looking at the "evidence for" and "evidence against" a schema will give you balanced thoughts.

In order to determine fact from distortion, refer to the list of common cognitive distortions on page 50–51 and see if any of them apply to the statements that are being considered as "evidence for." If they do apply, then the statement is a distortion, not a fact.

Identify a negative schema of yours:

_____

Complete the following table:

PROPOSED EVIDENCE THAT PROVES YOUR SCHEMA TO BE TRUE ("EVIDENCE FOR"):		
DO ANY COGNITIVE DISTORTIONS APPLY? IF SO, LIST THEM.		
ADD A CHECKMARK HERE IF THE STATEMENT WILL BE ADDED TO THE "EVIDENCE FOR" LIST, OR AN X IF IT'S NOT A FACT.		

List some facts that prove your schema to be false (evidence against):

_____

_____

_____

_____

_____

COMBATING COGNITIVE DISTORTIONS BY CHANGING THE WAY YOU THINK

Once you have identified your cognitive distortions and their related negative schemas, it's time to combat them using CBT techniques. Remember that CBT is based on the notion that thoughts determine feelings and behaviors. In order to change your automatic thoughts and schemas, you can use CBT techniques like decatastrophizing, dialectical thinking, and exploring balanced thoughts.

Decatastrophizing

Decatastrophizing is the process of facing the idea of the worst-case scenario, and concluding that what is most likely to happen is probably not as bad as one thinks. This is not to say that the situation won't cause any suffering. Instead, this process helps people realize that they'll be able to overcome any obstacles that come their way. People are capable of being resilient in the face of adversity, whether on their own or with some support. If a person views themself as resilient and capable of overcoming obstacles, then they are less likely to become angry.

Dialectical Thinking

Dialectical thinking is the process of looking at beliefs or situations from different perspectives and arriving upon the most factual and reasonable conclusion from an analysis of those perspectives. This type of thinking helps determine how true a schema is. When first starting to practice it, it may be helpful to use resources, such as journaling and CBT Thought Records (page 154–157). It may also be helpful to recruit a family member, friend, or therapist for an objective perspective. But eventually, and with lots of practice, it will be possible to use dialectical thinking without the help of external resources. This will help you regain emotional control during moments of anger.

Exploring Balanced Thoughts

Exploring balanced thoughts is key when it comes to challenging irrational schemas. When both positive and negative facts are included in the dialectical thinking process, it results in balanced thoughts. For example, suppose you struggle with the schema that "People are unreliable." You may try to dismiss it by telling yourself the positive fact: "I know there are instances that I have truly been able to rely on people." But this one-sided, positive thinking may not be enough to help you feel better. Positive thoughts don't make negative thoughts disappear. Negative thoughts will still linger unconsciously, unless they're acknowledged.

Here's an anecdote: Harriet is mad at her partner, Shay, for forgetting to wash the dishes again. Harriet recognizes that Shay is probably exhausted after a long day of work, so Harriet believes she shouldn't feel angry, and yet she does. Harriet identifies her schema as "I can't rely on anyone." She concludes with a balanced thought: "Although Shay has not been doing as many chores as I have, Shay does support me in other ways." This balanced thought helps Harriet address her negative and positive thoughts, so she feels less angry.

EXERCISE: DECATASTROPHIZING AND FINDING SOLUTIONS

When people catastrophize, they're fearing the worst-case scenario. They're not usually thinking about the likelihood of it coming to fruition, actions to reduce the likelihood of it happening, or coping skills for the aftermath. This keeps them stuck in their fears, which can lead to anger.

Write about a trigger that makes you angry because of catastrophizing. (e.g., *My partner asks me to do more for them in our relationship.*)

What are your worries? (e.g., *My partner isn't happy. My partner thinks I'm not committed to this relationship.*)

_____

_____

_____

Describe the worst-case scenario in your mind. (e.g., *My partner will cheat on me, I'll be devastated and angry, I'll become obsessed with learning about the person my partner cheated on me with, and I'll find and hurt them. Then I'll get caught and I'll be arrested.*)

_____

_____

_____

Identify any event in the catastrophized scenario that you'd like to explore and think about how likely it is to happen. To determine the likelihood, rate it on a scale of 1 to 10, with 1 being "not likely at all" and 10 being "extremely likely." A rating between 1 and 6 would mean it's not very likely to happen, while a rating between 7 and 10 would mean it's very likely to happen.

Event to explore (e.g., *My partner will cheat on me.*):

_____

Rating: _____   Very likely   Not very likely

If it is very likely to happen, list some reasonable actions you could take to reduce the chances of it happening.

For example:

Have regular check-ins with my partner about their happiness and relationship needs.

Discuss and agree to actions that will help us be more open and honest with each other.

_____

_____

_____

If there are no reasonable actions you could think of, then what are some healthy ways to cope with the aftermath (before the situation escalates) that will help you manage your anger?

For example:

Stay busy with healthy hobbies and spending time with people who actually care about me.

See a therapist to process it.

_____

_____

_____

If the event is not very likely to happen, what are the factors from which you drew that conclusion?

For example:

My partner tells me all the time that I make them happy.

My partner is overly honest.

My partner doesn't have the opportunity to cheat.

_____

_____

_____

EXERCISE: TURNING BLAME INTO SOLUTIONS

When you engage in blaming, you put yourself in a helpless position that can lead to anger. When you stop focusing on who to put the blame on, you'll be able to focus on problem-solving instead. Write out three anger-triggering situations and how you blamed yourself, others, or the circumstances. Then write about how you could have reduced blame and taken action toward a solution instead.

Here's an example:

Anger-triggering situation: My coworker took the credit for an idea I came up with.

Blame-related ideas: "It's my coworker's fault because they're so selfish." Or, "I don't speak up enough, so it's my fault." Or, "The universe just doesn't let me get ahead."

Ways I could have reduced blame and taken action:

→ Talk to my coworker about it.

→ During brainstorming meetings with this coworker, write out ideas we come up with in a follow-up email so that we have a paper trail.

→ Inform a supervisor if it becomes a pattern.

→ Look for a new job.

Anger-triggering situation:

_____

Blame-related ideas:

_____

Ways I could have reduced blame and taken action:

_____

Anger-triggering situation:

_____

Blame-related ideas:

_____

Ways I could have reduced blame and taken action:

_____

Anger-triggering situation:

_____

Blame-related ideas:

_____

Ways I could have reduced blame and taken action:

_____

Tyler

Tyler, now in his mid-20s, suffers from unhealthy anger toward men. When he was 6 years old, his older brother, Jake, who was 8 years old and very close to him at the time, suffered severe injuries in a car accident. The accident left Jake immobile and cognitively impaired. Tyler felt abandoned by his brother. In addition, because of the stress of his parents having to attend to Jake's new needs, along with work, financial constraints, and other responsibilities, Tyler's parents would often argue. Eventually, the arguments turned into physical abuse by his father against his mother. Tyler witnessed all this, and tried to defend his mom at times. His father would hit him, too, whenever he got in the way. Tyler felt alone, abandoned by his brother, and distrustful of his father. He also felt depressed and had low self-esteem.

As a young adult, he had several failed romantic relationships. He found himself staying too long in relationships with partners who abused him physically and emotionally. His resentment toward men grew. But because he lacked his father's love as a child, he also craved the love of a partner so much that he tolerated abusive treatment. At 25 years old, he started dating Ken. Ken was generally a respectful partner when sober, but when he was under the influence, he would get touchy-feely with others. Tyler felt insecure about this even though Ken never touched people inappropriately. One night, they were at a house party. At some point in the evening, Ken disappeared. When Tyler searched around, he found Ken in the bathroom lightly touching someone's shoulder while talking to them. When Tyler saw this, his automatic thoughts were: "Ken is cheating on me," "Ken brings out my jealous side," "Ken doesn't respect me," and "I'm feeling jealous so he must be doing something wrong." His schemas were "Men can't be trusted" and "No one will ever truly love me." The cognitive distortions related to his automatic thoughts were jumping to conclusions, blaming, and emotional reasoning.

As a result of these cognitive distortions, he screamed and physically attacked Ken and the other person. He lost control so much that Ken and his friends had to grab him and pin him down to the floor until he calmed down. Tyler felt deeply embarrassed by this, and Ken felt embarrassed to be with him. The next day, Ken broke up with Tyler.

COMBATING COGNITIVE DISTORTIONS BY CALMING YOUR MIND

When anger takes over, everything happens quickly. Because of the fight-or-flight mode, the mind focuses on whatever is threatening. As a result, negative ruminating thoughts take over and it may be difficult to challenge or let go of cognitive distortions. You can combat these distortions by shifting the focus to the physical senses or to positive thoughts. Mindfulness and relaxation techniques can help achieve this.

Mindfulness

Mindfulness is a practice that requires people to slow down and be present in the moment without judgment or interpretations of anything. This practice helps reduce negative thinking because it encourages people to have a neutral outlook about anything they experience. Mindfulness can be practiced independently, by engaging in creative or physical activities, or by connecting with others.

Some examples of independent mindfulness activities include focused meditation, mindful eating, and body scans. During focused meditation, people are instructed to focus on the different aspects of an object, including textures, smells, temperatures, and visual descriptors. During mindful eating, people focus on different aspects of the food they are eating (using as many physical senses as possible). During body scans, people focus on the sensations throughout their body.

Engaging in creative activities mindfully requires focus on the body's movements, use of tools, or visual appeal. Some examples of creative activities that can help you practice mindfulness include drawing, doodling, painting, cooking, origami, coloring, knitting, sewing, and dancing.

Mindful working out allows people to focus on their breathing, muscles, pain or discomfort, and body form. Some strength-based workouts include yoga, weight training, and CrossFit. Cardio workouts may include high-intensity interval training (HIIT), brisk walking, running, jumping rope, swimming, and rollerblading. Playing sports like tennis or basketball and mindfully practicing martial arts like tae kwon do and tai chi require focus on a person's position, body movements, goals and rules, defensive strategies, team communication, and pain from impact.

Daily activities that can also clear the mind include household chores and connecting with the outside world and others. Consider sitting outside your home or taking a long walk to lend your attention to people, animals, trees, buildings, or houses.

If you have young children, grandchildren, or pets, spending a little bit of time with them can give you a peek into a world through innocent eyes, which can not only give you a break from your own negative thoughts but can also help you to be more mindful in the scheme of things.

Relaxation Techniques

Aside from these mindfulness activities, there are relaxation techniques (e.g., meditation, left nostril breathing), some of which are covered throughout this book, that can help calm the mind and combat cognitive distortions. In addition, visualization and guided imagery can help the mind get to a relaxing place. Visualization is a technique that involves imagining a relaxing, safe, and happy place in detail. People delve into the visual experience by describing what their physical senses would be picking up while there. Guided imagery is similar to visualization, but the place is chosen by the speaker who is guiding the participant through it.

EXERCISE: MINDFULNESS

Use all your senses to practice mindfulness. As you answer the following prompts, try to be as objective as possible. Describe things as they are, and exclude any judgments about what you see. For example, if you see a messy desk, you can identify the different items on the desk. Don't judge it as "messy" or add anything about the reason it's messy.

Look in front of you. Describe what you see:

_____

_____

_____

_____

_____

_____

What do you smell?

_____

_____

_____

What do you hear? Cars? People? Your breathing? Nothing/silence?

_____

_____

_____

_____

_____

_____

What do you feel on your skin, lips, tongue, eyes, hair? Do you feel clothing, a hat, a breeze? What do you feel inside your body? The rise and fall of your breathing, a tingling sensation?

_____

_____

_____

_____

_____

_____

What do you taste? Any particular flavors? Or just bitter, sweet, sour, or salty?

_____

_____

_____

Anger Thermometer

Take a moment for self-care. Are you having any emotional triggers based on the topics discussed in this chapter? Any thoughts related to the examples described with the cognitive distortions? Any feelings related to having to think about worst-case scenarios when decatastrophizing? Did the stories bring up any triggers for you? Any triggers related to car accidents, domestic violence, abuse, embarrassment, or burning bridges out of anger?

Write about any triggers here, and if necessary, try the relaxation tip below.

_____

_____

_____

_____

_____

_____

_____

_____

Relaxation Tip: Smiling Meditation

Smiling in the same way you would when you're happy, even if you're not happy in the moment, can help activate your happy hormones. Try this smiling meditation whenever you're experiencing negative emotions.

1. Find a quiet place with minimal distractions.

2. Silence any devices that might interrupt you.

3. Close your eyes.

4. Sit up straight for optimal breathing.

5. Spread your feet shoulder-width apart and place your hands on your lap.

6. Slowly inhale through your nose, or mouth if you can't breathe through your nose.

7. As you slowly exhale, smile the same way you do when you're feeling happy, with your whole face.

8. Repeat the cycle five times.

CHAPTER TAKEAWAYS

→ Cognitive distortions are distorted ways of thinking that lead to negative automatic thoughts and schemas. By becoming familiar with them, you'll be more capable of identifying irrational thoughts and schemas so that you can challenge them.

→ Dialectical thinking is the process of looking at opinions or situations from different perspectives and arriving upon the most factual and reasonable conclusion from an analysis of those perspectives. This type of thinking helps determine how true a schema is.

→ When a schema is activated, people usually are only able to focus on the negative automatic thoughts that lend to it. Balanced thinking requires exploring the evidence that proves the schemas to be true, as well as evidence that proves it to be false.

→ In order to change your automatic thoughts and schemas, you can use CBT techniques such as decatastrophizing, dialectical thinking, and balanced thoughts. Mindfulness, visualization, and guided imagery can also help combat negative ruminating thoughts.

TAKE IT FORWARD

→ See if you can make mindfulness part of your daily routine. For the next few days, try practicing it for at least 15 minutes. Add a 15-minute block to your planner or calendar, use an alarm if that would be helpful, and practice mindfulness at the same time every day so that you're more likely to follow through. Giving your mind a break and simply being attuned to your senses for 15 minutes is one way to take control over your negative thoughts.

→ As you go about your day, make it a point to identify your automatic thoughts. If they're negative, explore the evidence that proves that they're true, as well as evidence that proves they're not true.

→ Practice balanced thinking. Remember the importance of looking at the whole picture. You don't want to focus only on the negative or positive. When you find yourself having negative thoughts, try to include both positive and negative facts. Write down these facts in your anger diary, and format them like this: "Although (negative fact), (positive fact)."

Unhealthy anger is not worth my time. My time, energy, and thoughts will be best dedicated to enjoyable experiences, environments, and people.

5

RESPONDING DIFFERENTLY

It's okay to be in touch with vulnerable emotions. Expressing my nonthreatening emotions will result in better communication.

This chapter focuses on understanding the vulnerable emotions that underlie anger. Emotional awareness can help individuals change the way they perceive situations. The chapter will continue with a discussion on regulating emotions and on managing physiological, emotional, and behavioral reactions. The exercises in the chapter will help increase your awareness of the consequences of unhealthy anger, build your empathy for others, improve your self-esteem, and brainstorm healthy distractions.

UNDERSTANDING YOUR EMOTIONS

Engaging more with your vulnerable emotions can help you change the way you think and act during moments that usually trigger your anger. Some examples of vulnerable emotions include sadness, depression, helplessness, hopelessness, worry, embarrassment, guilt, and shame. Vulnerable emotions don't typically activate the "fight" reaction from the sympathetic nervous system (SNS) that exists with anger. Because the resulting behaviors from vulnerable emotions are nonthreatening, people on the receiving end of a communication are more likely to respond positively to these types of emotions, and this leads to better communication.

If you could identify your vulnerable emotions during a moment of anger, then you could express those emotions instead of anger. This would allow you to behave differently than you would with anger. You could calmly problem-solve by seeking clarification, weighing options, and working on changing the way you communicate.

Here's an anecdote to further explain. Lyn feels angry because her very good friend Jan likes to joke about depression. Lyn has several family members who suffer from depression, so she feels this is insensitive. It angers her that some people think it's funny to joke about a mental illness that could actually lead people to take their own lives. If Lyn isn't in touch with her vulnerable emotions, she's more likely to feel angry and react to Jan's jokes. She might either avoid Jan altogether, make a passive-aggressive comment (using a sarcastic tone: "Wow, you're so funny."), be actively aggressive in confronting her ("You really think that's funny?"), or offend her ("You're really ignorant for thinking it's okay to joke about this.").

These angry reactions would have negative consequences for Lyn. They could lead to an argument, embarrassment, an end to the friendship, and burned bridges.

If, by contrast, Lyn takes some time to explore her underlying vulnerable emotions, she might realize that what she feels underneath her anger is hurt and sad. The thought related to these vulnerable emotions might be "People don't understand how serious depression is." Her vulnerable feelings would not activate her SNS, and would instead allow her the capacity and time to think of solutions instead of feeling helpless and emotionally threatened.

EXERCISE: VULNERABLE EMOTIONS
THAT UNDERLIE ANGER

It's important to be in touch with your vulnerable emotions so that you can express these nonaggressive emotions instead of anger. Look at the following list of vulnerable emotions. Then add any others you can think of on the blank lines.

Sad	**Scared**	**Hopeless**
Upset	**Ashamed**	**Helpless**
Disappointed	**Worthless**	**Disrespected**
Tired	**Betrayed**	**Judged**
Overwhelmed	**Hurt**	_____
Worried	**Abandoned**	_____

Now list some anger-triggering situations and the underlying vulnerable emotions:

Situation:

_____

_____

_____

Emotion(s):

_____

Situation:

_____

_____

_____

Emotion(s):

_____

Situation:

_____

_____

_____

Emotion(s):

_____

Situation:

_____

_____

_____

Emotion(s):

_____

EXERCISE: EMOTION RATING PRACTICE

It's important to get a sense of how intense your negative emotions are at any given moment. Increasing awareness of your emotional intensity can help you take a step back and look at upsetting situations objectively. Doing so will help you use your rational brain (frontal lobes) to respond to your anger.

Read through the following scenarios, consider what emotions they would spark, and rate the intensity of those emotions. The ratings in this exercise are on a scale of 1 to 10. One means the emotion is very mild, 5 means the emotion is moderate, and 10 means the emotion is extremely intense. After going through the scenarios included in the table, fill in your own scenarios, emotions, and emotion ratings.

STATEMENT/SITUATION	EMOTIONS	EMOTION RATING
On the way to work, the lunch that I was looking forward to eating fell out of my bag and splattered all over the sidewalk.		
Traffic made me late for work again.		
My child had a temper tantrum at the checkout line. We were going to buy all the groceries we needed for the week, but we had to leave the store empty-handed.		
On a hot day, I was craving ice cream after getting home. I saw the tub of ice cream in the freezer. I got a spoon, opened it, and it was empty.		

Syd

Syd, now in his 30s, has anxiety that manifests as anger. When Syd was a child, his father worked long hours and became an alcoholic as a result of the stress. Syd's mother cheated on his father, and Syd found out. This news hurt Syd because he was protective of his father.

Syd didn't have the best relationship with his mother. When Syd was a teenager, his mom would call him "weak" and "scrawny." She would tell him that no one was going to like him because he didn't work out. When he became interested in girls, he struggled to find someone interested in him. It made him feel badly about himself. In his early 20s, he started dating someone. A few months in, she told him she just didn't feel like being with him anymore, and so she left him. In his mid-20s, he met someone else; however, she was emotionally abusive. This relationship brought out his anger because he felt helpless. They would often have screaming matches because she wouldn't listen when he spoke calmly. They broke up after two years.

A few years later, he met someone else. She was much calmer and passive. They never had an argument in the four years of their relationship, until they were engaged and planning their wedding. The wedding planning led to many disagreements. The arguments triggered Syd's schemas: "Women will easily abandon me because I can't make them happy," "Women cheat when they're unhappy," and "Women are critical." These schemas and triggers led to automatic thoughts such as "She's not listening to me," "She doesn't care about how I want our wedding to be," and "She doesn't respect my opinion on the wedding decisions." The frequent activation of these negative schemas and automatic thoughts eventually led to Syd having an anger outburst, which resulted in his fiancée ending the relationship.

Syd's experiences with women (including his mother) affected him emotionally. He "learned" that women cheat. That women are critical of him and will eventually leave him, even if things are going well. That women don't respect him and his decisions. That women need to be yelled at when they don't listen to him.

Eventually, he met someone else who he married. His schemas led him to become triggered frequently and therefore affected his marriage. They went to couples counseling, which helped him feel safe in their relationship. In therapy, Syd explored his underlying vulnerable emotions, practiced openly expressing them to his partner, and learned ways to regulate them. This helped improve their marriage significantly.

EMOTIONAL REGULATION

Emotional regulation, also known as "affect regulation," is the ability to manage emotions. Regulating strong negative emotions is an important component of anger management, and there are several ways to do so: being solution focused, working on schemas, and having healthy emotional hygiene.

Being Solution Focused

When people handle situations with a solution-focused perspective, stressors don't have as great of an impact on emotions, so they're easier to manage. Although problems don't always get resolved in the way people want, they are ultimately still getting resolved. Being open to different resolutions, even when they're not ideal, is helpful when trying to have a solution-focused mentality. Depending on the problem, it's best to think of either the most efficient resolution or the one that will yield better long-term results. In addition, thinking about how good it will feel once the problem is solved can be helpful. When people focus on problems, it can make them miserable.

Take this example: Your roommate dropped a large container of yogurt on the kitchen floor by accident, had to rush out of the house for an appointment, apologized profusely, and asked you the huge favor of cleaning it up. The thoughts you choose to have in this situation will determine how you feel. You could choose to focus on how cleaning will take up precious time that you could be spending doing something else, or the fear that your roommate will continue to make messes often because of their carelessness. These thoughts would probably make you feel annoyed or angry. Instead, if you focus on getting it done right away and later addressing the clumsiness in a calm conversation with your roommate, then you're less likely to ruminate about negative concerns. Focusing on solutions will keep your mood light and result in reduced suffering.

Working on Schemas

Working on one's own schemas can help with affect regulation. Schemas determine how people view themselves, others, the world, and the future. So, if a person's schemas are positive, then they'll have a positive outlook, and this will help them make positive assumptions. Positive schemas would allow them to give others the benefit of the doubt and would reduce the chances of feeling offended, reacting defensively, or becoming angry.

Awareness of one's own negative schemas can help predict emotional or physical discomfort. It will allow them to think of solutions before they encounter triggers. For example, if Person A knows their anger tends to be triggered around Person B because of the schema "Person B doesn't care about me," then Person A might consider working on this schema by using some preparatory empathy before facing Person B. Preparatory empathy means putting oneself in another person's shoes for a moment, shortly before interacting with them. By empathizing with others, people are more likely to be patient and less likely to become angry.

Healthy Emotional Hygiene

Another way to improve your affect regulation is by improving your emotional hygiene. When you're feeling well emotionally, your mind can be clear of negativity and therefore make it easier to regulate your emotions. Negative emotions and thoughts need healthy outlets. If they're not expressed in healthy ways, they may eventually come out at the wrong time, around the wrong people, and in an unhealthy way. They could manifest as passive or active aggression. Some healthy outlets include journaling, CBT Thought Records (page 154–157), reaching out to loved ones or online communities on social media for support, and connecting with a therapist.

EXERCISE: PREPARATORY EMPATHY

Think about the people who tend to trigger your anger. The next time you're about to interact with them, consider preparatory empathy. Complete the following prompts for one or two people in your life, to help you develop preparatory empathy.

Someone who tends to trigger my anger: _____

_____

_____

Things they do that annoy or anger me:

_____

_____

_____

If I'm giving them the benefit of the doubt, what can explain why they behave the way they do?

_____

_____

_____

Someone who tends to trigger my anger: _____

Things they do that annoy or anger me:

_____

_____

_____

If I'm giving them the benefit of the doubt, what can explain why they behave the way they do?

_____

_____

_____

EXERCISE: LIST THE CONSEQUENCES
OF UNHEALTHY ANGER

Create a list of past, current, and possible future consequences of unhealthy anger in your life, sorted by categories. Write it out here, and again on a sticky note, a virtual note in your phone, and/or in your anger diary for easy reference.

Romantic life (loneliness, toxic relationships, abandonment, etc.):

_____

_____

_____

Social life (relationships with loved ones, daily interactions, short- and long-term impact, etc.):

_____

_____

_____

Work life (keeping your job, relationships with coworkers, being respected by your colleagues, etc.):

_____

_____

_____

Mental well-being (depression, guilt, loneliness, shame, anxiety, negative moods, irritability, etc.):

_____

_____

_____

Physical well-being (medical issues, fatigue, nutrition, appetite, sleep quality, physical activity, etc.):

_____

_____

_____

MANAGING YOUR REACTIONS

When people struggle with anger, they must learn to manage their emotional, physiological, and behavioral reactions. Some ways to do this include having a positive attitude, being aware of emotional red flags and physiological warning signs, increasing awareness of the consequences of anger reactions, having a healthy lifestyle, and taking space away from stressors.

Having a generally positive attitude can help positive emotions become the norm so that negative emotions turn into red flags. Being more aware of emotional red flags can help people notice them during stressful moments and therefore manage negative emotions before they escalate. Some ways to foster a positive attitude include: being physically healthy (including a healthy diet, adequate sleep, and exercises that release "happy hormones"), surrounding oneself with positive and encouraging people, establishing and maintaining healthy relationships, and engaging in enjoyable activities.

Another way to manage anger reactions is to increase awareness of one's physiological warning signs. Being aware of one's own physiological changes helps people become more capable of reducing their body tension during moments of anger. Reducing body tension is one way to help deactivate the sympathetic nervous system so that people can respond to their anger, instead of react. Two techniques to help increase awareness of the body include progressive relaxation and strength-based exercises. Progressive relaxation is a technique that entails intentionally tensing and relaxing different muscle groups in order to help people become aware of tense and relaxed states. Strength training exercises can help in a similar way, by requiring people to focus on different muscle groups at a time.

It's important also to keep in mind the consequences of the emotional, physiological, and behavioral reactions that come with unhealthy anger. Remember that your reactions can cause issues with your social life, work life, mental and physical well-being, and livelihood. When you keep the consequences of unhealthy anger at the forefront of your mind, you become less likely to behave in ways that would result in those consequences.

Maintaining a healthy lifestyle can help with managing anger reactions because it typically results in increased energy and positive hormones. When people feel energized, the brain has the resources to manage anger reactions. Increased positive hormones make it more likely to think positively, which can contribute to positive schemas and a solution-focused mentality. A healthy lifestyle includes attending to health issues, taking care of the body's physiological needs (such as nutrition and sleep), and having a healthy amount of social interaction (more on this topic in chapter 8).

Of course, there will be times when a person won't be able to manage their behaviors, negative emotions, or physiological reactions. The anger may escalate so quickly that they won't be able to slow down, empathize with themselves or others, or problem-solve. In these situations, clear communication is rarely successful. This is why it's best to distance oneself from the stressor for a limited time period, try some relaxation techniques, and/or explore and challenge negative automatic thoughts.

EXERCISE: USING HEALTHY DISTRACTIONS

Healthy distractions can give the mind and body a break during moments of anger. They can help reduce ruminating thoughts and turn off the fight-or-flight response. Engaging in healthy distractions is a CBT technique that can help change the way you feel and/or think about a situation. Here's a list of healthy distractions. Check off the ones you want to try. Feel free to engage in any of these for the amount of time that you prefer, as long as they don't interfere with your ability to function or your responsibilities.

→   Taking a brisk walk outside

→   Taking a slow walk outside

→   Sewing

→   Knitting

→ Cross-stitching

→ Sketching

→ Drawing

→ Baking

→ Origami

→ Coloring

→ Tracing lines in a book with complex geometrical designs

→ Dancing by yourself or with a loved one

→ Engaging in visualization or guided imagery

→ Working on a puzzle

→ Watching a quick video from a comedian

→ Playing with a pet

→ Looking at photos or videos of cute animals

→ Calling someone to check in on how they're doing

→ Calling or messaging a friend who always makes you laugh

After you try out a couple of these, journal about your experiences.

EXERCISE: HAVING A HEALTHY SELF-ESTEEM

A healthy self-esteem will reduce your chances of becoming angry at yourself, help you feel less easily offended, and allow you to see others in a positive light. Look through this checklist of positive qualities and check off those that apply to you. If you need help with this exercise, consider asking someone who is fond of you: "What are some things you like about me?" Or, you can try to imagine what they might say. Don't be afraid to be kind to yourself! Self-acceptance is necessary in order to overcome anger. Keep in mind that positive qualities don't always apply to all situations and areas in life, so if you possess a quality in one area, then this is part of who you are and should contribute to how you see yourself. For example, if you're a funny person around your friends but struggle with being this way around new crowds, you should still check off "funny" as a quality.

I am:

- → Smart
- → Creative
- → Funny
- → Good at/with

  _____

- → Good at/with

  _____

- → Honest
- → Kind

  _____

  _____

- → Humble
- → Friendly
- → Helpful
- → Good at my job
- → A good student
- → Driven
- → Strong

  _____

  _____

Now take your descriptors and write them out in a statement:

I am: _____

Read this statement aloud to yourself in the mirror. Throughout your anger management journey, refer to it often to give you a boost when you're feeling down.

Anger Thermometer

Take a moment for self-care. Are you having any emotional triggers based on the topics covered in this chapter? Any thoughts related to expressing vulnerable emotions? Did the story bring up any triggers for you? Did any of the examples in the exercises trigger negative emotions? Any triggers from listing the consequences of unhealthy anger in your life?

Write about any triggers here, and if necessary, try the relaxation tip below.

_____

_____

_____

_____

_____

Relaxation Tip: Soothe Yourself with Soothing Sounds

Everyone has different preferences on the types of sounds that help them feel relaxed. Before listening to the sounds, try to find a quiet place with minimal distractions and either sit up straight or lie down. While you listen to the sounds, try practicing deep, slow breathing. You can try relaxing music or relaxing sounds like the rain, beach waves, a river, or birds chirping. You can try white noise (a consistent set of tones that are played in tandem and at the same intensity), or other variations such as pink, blue, or brown noise. Or maybe you'll find it helpful to hear a person's voice. You can try a sleep story or a podcast with a speaker who has a soothing voice. All of these options are available through different apps or online.

CHAPTER TAKEAWAYS

→ Unhealthy anger prevents people from communicating clearly.

→ Being in touch with the vulnerable emotions that underlie a person's anger can help change thoughts and behaviors in a way that will allow for clarity in communication.

→ You can enhance your emotional regulation by being solution focused, working on schemas, and having healthy emotional hygiene.

→ Building empathy for others can help reduce anger. It helps with seeing the innocent and good intentions of others.

→ Improving one's self-esteem is helpful because when a person feels good about themselves, they're less likely to make negative assumptions about how people see them.

→ You can manage physiological, emotional, and behavioral reactions with a positive attitude, being aware of your physiological reactions, keeping the consequences of unhealthy anger in mind, and living a healthy lifestyle.

TAKE IT FORWARD

→ Read your list of anger consequences aloud and set reminders to refer to the list every two days this week.

→ Looking at yourself and others in a positive light will help you feel happier and calmer. Practice making positive comments about yourself and others.

  → Compliment someone you interact with in the next few days. Try to focus on their personality, values, or behavior, as opposed to their physical appearance.

  → Write about any efforts you made to accomplish things throughout the day, regardless of whether or not you were successful. People can't control results but they can control their efforts.

  → Try to avoid or reduce negative language such as name-calling when talking about yourself or others. Using positive language to describe yourself and others can help build your self-esteem and empathy, which will help with managing your anger reactions.

→ Practice being aware of how often you feel offended by others or the circumstances. Is there another way of viewing these situations so that you don't feel like the world is against you?

I will become more aware of my negative thinking patterns. I will take control over them by engaging in relaxation techniques, enjoyable activities, and healthy distractions.

6

HANDLING CONFLICTS AND COMMUNICATION ISSUES

Misunderstandings happen all the time. When I notice myself experiencing negative emotions, I will try to first assume that there is a misunderstanding that needs to be clarified.

This chapter focuses on healthy and productive communication. It will cover: "I" statements, assertiveness, nonverbal communication, barriers to healthy communication, boundary setting, and healthy conflict resolution, and will present exercises to help you practice healthy and effective communication.

HEALTHY AND PRODUCTIVE COMMUNICATION

Unhealthy anger can cloud communication because the emotional brain takes over. It can make others feel scared or threatened, or it can make someone seem like a different person altogether. Unhealthy anger makes people focus on their feelings of helplessness and the perceived need to fight threats. This causes people to be on attack mode rather than listening mode, so they won't be able to pay attention to others during communication. Healthy communication requires active listening and an open mind. So, when people are stuck in an anger-induced negative thought loop, their efforts to communicate are unproductive. In order to get out of this negative mindset and be a good listener and communicator, individuals must focus on feelings of empowerment and the desire to find solutions. Establishing new, healthy, and honest communication patterns is essential.

Honesty about how a person feels when triggered is an important part of overcoming unhealthy anger. When people lack honesty with themselves and others, negative emotions are more likely to develop and worsen, and misunderstandings occur with no resolution in sight. Without honesty, people can't take action to understand what is actually happening in a situation. By acknowledging and addressing their own concerns, people give themselves the opportunity to challenge their negative beliefs and resolve misunderstandings.

Here's an anecdote to explain further. Jen wants to feel confident in her open relationship, but actually feels insecure about it. She tries to tell herself that she shouldn't feel insecure, and that she doesn't really care if her partner has intimate experiences with other people. But when her partner tells her about a recent intimate experience with someone else, she becomes angry. She chooses to keep these thoughts and feelings to herself, which results in her anger worsening. She acts passive aggressively and aloof toward her partner when they tell her about their experiences with other people, and this leaves her partner confused and hurt. The next time her partner tells her about an intimate experience, she's unable to remain calm anymore and has an anger outburst.

Jen's insecurities and helplessness transformed to anger. Had she been honest with herself about the fact that she felt insecure, she might have prevented the anger outburst. Acknowledging the reality could have sprung her into action by journaling about it, or discussing it with a friend and/or her partner. She would have been able to find the words to calmly express how she really felt about the situation, and this would have helped her feel empowered.

EXERCISE: EXPLORING SOLUTIONS

When it comes to healthy communication and conflict resolution, it's important to practice exploring solutions. You can explore solutions on your own, with the help of loved ones, through the use of social media, or by presenting your concerns in online community forums.

For this exercise, think about a recent problem that led to anger. List the factors that were beyond your control, and then list the factors and actions that were within your control. And the next time you have a problem that's making you feel helpless and angry, try using this format to brainstorm in your anger diary.

Here's an example:

Anger trigger: My friend went out of their way to elaborately lie to me and other friends in our circle.

The problem: I won't ever be able to trust them again.

What is beyond your control:

→   Making them become honest

Possible solutions/what is within your control:

→   I can end the friendship

→   I can stay friends with them but not be as close and take everything they say with caution

Write about an anger trigger:

_____

_____

Describe the problem:

_____

_____

What is beyond your control?

_____

_____

_____

Possible solutions: What is within your control?

_____

_____

_____

EXERCISE: USING "I" STATEMENTS

"I" statements involve the use of the words "I" or "we." They help the listener feel less blamed or attacked and therefore lead to more open communication. When using "I" statements, communication is more focused on the speaker's experience rather than on the listener. Read the following tips on using "I" statements and then complete the mix and match exercise.

→   Focus on your own experience instead of the other person's behavior or words.

→   Comment on the impact of the problem on yourself.

→   Instead of "your," use "the," "this," or "an."

→   Use "we" instead of "you."

→   Avoid blaming or making accusations.

→   Express vulnerable emotions as opposed to threatening emotions like annoyance, anger, irritability, or frustration.

"I" Statements Mix and Match

Draw a line from a negative statement on the left to the matching "I" statement on the right.

NEGATIVE STATEMENTS	"I" STATEMENTS
You're attacking me.	I haven't had lunch yet so I'm a bit cranky.
You're getting on my nerves.	I'm feeling exhausted and unable to communicate well right now.
You care about everyone else but me.	I feel like I'm being attacked.
You're exhausting to deal with.	I feel like I'm not being prioritized.

Now try converting the following negative statements to "I" statements:

Negative statement: You're basically calling me dumb.

"I" statement: _____

Negative statement: You're annoying me.

"I" statement: _____

Negative statement: You made me mad when you rolled your eyes.

"I" statement: _____

Negative statement: You don't care about me.

"I" statement: _____

UNDERSTANDING ASSERTIVENESS

Assertiveness is an important skill for managing anger because it's the most effective way to communicate one's emotions and needs. It's a way to communicate that involves clear, direct, respectful, and nonthreatening communication. It helps people address emotional threats by expressing their concerns and needs in a healthy way. As a result, it helps build trust in relationships and reduces the incidence of anger.

Here are a couple of examples of assertive statements:

→ "This topic is making me nervous. Can we talk about something else?"

→ "I'm really trying to reduce the use of foul language around my kids, and I find cursing to be contagious. Would you please try not to curse as much around me?"

Notice how each statement includes what is being requested and the reason for the request. When people understand the reasons behind a request, they're more likely to empathize rather than become defensive.

Keep in mind that when it comes to communicating, people don't just communicate with their words. They communicate with their nonverbal language such as body posture and positioning, tone of voice, eye contact, and hand gestures. Look back to the previous examples of assertive statements. Imagine saying them with an aggressive tone or body language. How do you think people would feel and respond to this type of nonverbal language? They would likely feel upset and react defensively. What about the message you're trying to communicate? Do you think they would receive your message as intended? Or would they mostly respond to your nonverbal cues instead?

Consider this anecdote. Gil is in a relationship with Hope. Gil gets angry often because he assumes Hope is being selfish (this is one of his schemas). In the past, whenever he became upset, he would keep his emotions to himself and eventually boil over into anger. So now he wants to try a new approach, which is to use relaxation techniques and assertiveness. During stressful situations, he tries to stay as calm as possible by using deep-breathing techniques. If the relaxation techniques aren't enough to keep him in a neutral or good mood, he speaks up assertively. During an outing one day, Hope couldn't make up her mind on what to eat. Gil started thinking that she wasn't being considerate about the fact that he was hungry. Because of this automatic thought, he noticed his frustration building. So, he softly touched her arm, made eye contact with her, and calmly said: "Honey, I'm so glad to be here with you. We've been sitting for a while now and have yet to place our orders. I want to be patient with you but my hunger is getting in the way. Is there anything I can do to help you decide?" Because of this direct communication, Hope makes her decision right away and they're able to enjoy the rest of their outing.

EXERCISE: VISUALIZE HEALTHY CONFRONTATION

Nonaggressive confrontation is one component of clear, open, and assertive communication, and can help you connect with others. You may be hesitant about confronting people because you want to avoid tension. Maybe you worry about losing emotional control. Or perhaps you worry that the other person might react aggressively or feel hurt. In order to get past these concerns, consider visualizing the conversation and practicing what you might say. You can do this on your own through journaling or with the help of others by discussing and rehearsing with them.

Identify a person with whom you had or currently have an issue that triggered negative emotions, but weren't or aren't comfortable confronting them about it:

_____

Identify the issue(s) you're upset or angry about:

_____

_____

_____

If you were to confront this person about the issue, how might they react or respond?

_____

_____

_____

List any assumptions you might make about their words, behavior, or body language:

_____

_____

_____

In what ways could you seek clarification of your assumptions?

_____

_____

_____

How can you make this confrontation as gentle as possible? Write out what you might say using these tips.

→ Use "I" statements.

→ Use the "criticism sandwich": Start with something positive, give your criticism, and end with another positive comment.

→ Focus on the positive.

→ Focus on solutions rather than problems.

_____

_____

EXERCISE: SEEKING CLARIFICATION

It's important to seek clarification when you find yourself feeling offended. Most of the time, people aren't trying to hurt your feelings. And if they are, it's usually because they themselves feel hurt, too. Seeking clarification can help you empathize with others, get past misunderstandings, reduce negative thoughts, and reduce your anger as a result.

Consider these tips when seeking clarification:

→ Avoid "why" questions, because they tend to make people become defensive.

→ Avoid accusations. You're more likely to be met with a defensive attitude when you make accusations.

→ Avoid asking for anything from others until after you get clarification. People are more likely to listen when they are given the opportunity to speak first.

→ If necessary, after getting clarification, you can suggest that _____ not be said or done again.

→ Use passive language such as:

→ "It sounds like . . ."

→ "It seems like . . ."

→ "I think I heard you say . . ."

→ Use "I" statements.

→ Express your vulnerable emotions instead of your aggressive emotions.

Here are some examples of ways to seek clarification:

Example 1

Situation:

I went out to dinner with some friends, and we split the bill equally even though one of my friends felt that was unfair. The next day I felt badly about it, so I refunded some of their money to reflect the part of the bill that was for them only. They never acknowledged it.

Anger-related thoughts: They're unappreciative. They're spiteful. They're trying to hurt my feelings.

Vulnerable emotions: Hurt, unappreciated

How I could have sought clarification: I can ask them if they received the money. If they did, then I could explain my reason for sending it. If they still don't acknowledge my gesture, then I can say, "Honestly, I am feeling a bit unappreciated as a friend. I tried to do something nice for you but it wasn't acknowledged."

Example 2

Situation:

My friend told me they had a small 20-person elopement and didn't even think to invite me. I had invited them to my wedding when I got married.

Anger-related thoughts: They don't value me. They're rude.

Vulnerable emotions: Confused, sad

How I could have sought clarification: "I'm really happy for you, but we're good friends, so I honestly expected an invitation."

Example 3

Situation:

I started dating someone and, without even meeting them, my friend told me I could do better.

Anger-related thoughts: They think I have poor judgment. They think I'm desperate.

Vulnerable emotions: Hurt, offended

How I could have sought clarification: "It feels like I'm being viewed as having poor judgment or being desperate."

Now you try it. Write about some situations where you made negative assumptions and didn't seek clarification. What words could you have used to seek clarification in an assertive way?

Situation:

_____

_____

_____

Anger-related thoughts:

_____

_____

Vulnerable emotions:

_____

_____

_____

How I could have sought clarification:

_____

_____

_____

Situation:

_____

_____

_____

Anger-related thoughts:

_____

_____

_____

Vulnerable emotions:

_____

_____

_____

How I could have sought clarification:

_____

_____

_____

Shylo

Shylo, now in his late 60s, is a lonely empty nester who has dealt with anger issues for most of his life. During his childhood, his father was abusive and suffered from alcoholism. His mother abandoned him because she wanted to get away from the abuse and wasn't ready for parenthood in her early 20s. As a result, he was placed in foster care and transferred between many homes. In those homes, he underwent emotional and physical abuse by his foster parents, and was often bullied by his foster siblings. He felt unloved and unwanted. He felt insecure in all his relationships, with a deep underlying fear that people would abandon him (like his mom) and that he was incapable of being loved (because he never felt his father's or anyone else's love). This led to loneliness and anger. When he turned 20, he started dating a peer who was also in the foster care system. A few months into dating her, she became pregnant. He felt excited by the pregnancy because he thought this was an opportunity to finally be loved unconditionally (by his child).

Unfortunately, Shylo struggled with patience as a partner and father. He had never learned the skills necessary to be good at these roles, which are to communicate clearly and to be able to resolve conflicts in a calm manner. Whenever his child, Ary, didn't do as they were told, Shylo would yell at them. Whenever Shylo and his partner disagreed on something, he would get angry and yell at her.

Had Shylo known how to communicate assertively, he would not have felt the need to communicate aggressively. So, when Ary didn't do as they were told, Shylo could have lowered himself down to Ary's eye level and used a stern voice to ensure that Ary was paying attention. If Ary still disregarded Shylo's directives, then Shylo could implement nonaggressive consequences like a time-out or taking privileges or items away. Healthy conflict resolution could also have helped his relationship. During conflicts, Shylo could have used CBT communication techniques such as seeking clarification, being honest about how he feels, and taking space to calm down.

RESOLVING CONFLICTS

Unresolved conflicts can cause helplessness and eventually become emotional threats that lead to anger; therefore, it's important to learn healthy conflict resolution. Conflicts can be resolved internally or externally. Conflicts that are resolved internally don't involve confrontation of the person who triggered the negative emotions. Conflicts that are resolved externally involve confronting the person who triggered the negative emotions.

Conflicts can be resolved internally through:

→ Calming your mind (healthy distractions, distancing from stressors, diaphragmatic breathing, mindfulness, visualization, guided imagery, meditation)

→ CBT journaling techniques (thought records, listing and challenging negative automatic thoughts and schemas, listing cognitive distortions, listing balanced thoughts)

→ Self-esteem building (affirmations, focusing on positive characteristics)

→ Empathy building (preparatory empathy, giving the benefit of the doubt)

→ Keeping the consequences of unhealthy anger in mind

→ Having a solution-focused mentality

→ Dialectical thinking, either on your own or by discussing with others

Conflicts can be resolved externally through:

→ Productive communication techniques (assertiveness, healthy boundary setting, communicating emotions and thoughts, being honest with yourself and others, seeking clarification, using "I" statements)

→ Using gentle physical touch where appropriate

→ Agreeing to give each other space for a limited time when either person is not ready to communicate

→ Communicating through written means such as letters, text, or email

Here's an anecdote. Matt, who lives with Fae, usually makes the bed every morning. Matt doesn't really care whether the bed is made or not, but has decided to be responsible for it because he knows it makes Fae happy. Recently, however, he's been out of the house a lot caring for his sick parent, so he hasn't had time to make the bed. After the fifth day of the bed not being made, Fae notices this is becoming a pattern and becomes upset and tense. She tries resolving it internally at first by keeping in mind the fact that Matt is very busy and going through a rough time. She identifies her schema (*He doesn't care about my happiness*) and comes up with balanced thoughts (*Although he hasn't made the bed in the last few days, he's always made the bed previously. Although he hasn't taken me out on a date in a few weeks, he's ordered dinner from my favorite restaurants a few times*). Processing this conflict internally was helpful because she didn't feel as upset and tense as she did before processing it. Still, she feels it necessary to bring it up to him (externalizing) because she sees the fact that he didn't ask for help as a problem that may lead to other issues in the future. She calmly tells him: "My love, I know you've been busy, but it only takes a few minutes to make the bed. When I go into the room, I expect the bed to be made because you always make it. If there's no time for you to make it, please just ask for my help." Matt apologized and agreed to be better about communicating in the future.

Although conflict resolution can be extremely helpful for anger management, not all issues need to be addressed (internally or externally). Sometimes just giving yourself some time away from stressors and/or using healthy distractions or relaxation techniques can be enough. But if negative thoughts and emotions persist and interfere with your life after having some space away from the stressor, addressing them internally or externally will help reduce the incidence of unhealthy anger.

EXERCISE: USING CLEAR COMMUNICATION

Anger can surface when your needs aren't being met. In order to have your needs met, however, you need to communicate them clearly. It's important to use clear communication to speak up before vulnerable emotions become anger. Complete this exercise to practice learning about clear versus unclear communication.

Clear communication involves:

→ Keeping calm

→ Using "I" statements

→ Explicitly verbalizing your vulnerable emotions

→ If necessary, directly asking for what you need

Read through each statement and write in "clear" or "unclear" in the lines to the left.

_____ I told my sibling I was angry.

_____ I stayed quiet the whole time because I was upset.

_____ I raised my voice because the conversation was stressful.

_____ I told my parents that I feel hurt because I was lied to (by them).

_____ I raised my eyebrows because I was shocked at the offensive remark my friend made.

answers: clear; unclear; unclear; clear; unclear.

Now read the issue examples below and write a sentence that would communicate emotions and/or needs clearly. Then add your own issue and "clear communication" example.

Issue: My friend made an offensive comment about a group of people I identify with.

Clear Communication:

_____

Issue: My aunt is gloating about having just bought a home, knowing that my home purchasing deal just fell through.

Clear Communication:

_____

Issue:

_____

Clear Communication:

_____

EXERCISE: LEARNING ASSERTIVENESS

When people don't set healthy boundaries, they're more likely to feel helpless and angry. People can't read minds, and many don't read social cues very well. Therefore, it's best not to assume that people will pay attention to nonverbal cues.

If you need something, don't expect others to be attuned to those needs. Try these tips when speaking up for yourself. Afterward, review the example and complete the exercise.

→   Be confident with what you're saying or requesting.

→   Use a calm and caring tone and body language.

　→   Avoid crossed arms or furrowed brows.

　→   Avoid standing above the other person.

　→   Make a healthy amount of direct eye contact.

→ Make positive comments. If you don't have any positive thoughts about the situation, give the other person the benefit of the doubt. Imagine what positive intentions they may have. Examples:

  → "It was lovely talking to you!"

  → "So glad you called."

→ Use positive language.

  → "I do need to . . ." instead of "I can't do . . ."

  → Example: "I do have to get off the phone because I have to read a book to my child." instead of "I can't be on the phone."

→ Use "I" statements

  → Example: "I'm glad we're outside right now but I am feeling hot and have to go back inside so that I don't get cranky from the heat."

Example:
Situation where I didn't speak up until I became angry: My cousin kept talking to me on the phone and I had some important material I needed to read. I didn't yell at them but now I'm angry at them for taking up my time.

Barriers to setting healthy boundaries: I didn't want to make them feel bad by interrupting them.

Ways to problem-solve/actions I can take: The next time I need to get off the phone, I'll say "I'm really sorry for interrupting but I do need to get off the phone right now." I'll let them know that I'll try to call them back as soon as I can. If they don't let me get a word in, I will say, "Oh, I'm sorry but I have to take this call! I'll try my best to call you back. Nice talking with you!"

Now it's your turn to try:

Situation where I didn't speak up until I became angry:

_____

_____

_____

Barriers to setting healthy boundaries:

_____

_____

_____

Ways to problem-solve/actions I can take:

_____

_____

_____

Anger Thermometer

Take a moment for self-care. Are you having any emotional triggers based on the topics discussed in this chapter? Did the stories bring up any triggers for you? Any thoughts about loneliness, insecurities, abandonment, or negative experiences in foster care? What about anger affecting the emotional and mental well-being of others? Did any of the examples in the exercises trigger negative emotions?

Write about any triggers here, and if necessary, try the relaxation tip below.

_____

_____

_____

_____

Relaxation Tip: Square Breathing

1. Find a quiet place with minimal distractions.

2. Silence any devices that might interrupt you.

3. Close your eyes.

4. Sit up straight for optimal breathing.

5. Spread your feet shoulder-width apart and place your hands on your lap.

6. Slowly inhale for 4 seconds through your nose, or mouth if you can't breathe through your nose.

7. Hold your breath for 4 seconds.

8. Exhale for 4 seconds through your mouth.

9. Hold your breath for 4 seconds.

10. Repeat steps 6 to 9 several times until you feel relaxed.

CHAPTER TAKEAWAYS

→ Being honest with yourself and others will help you feel less angry. Honesty will allow you to explore your automatic thoughts and schemas, challenge them if necessary, and/or communicate them in a healthy way.

→ Assertiveness is vital to anger management. It is a form of communicating that involves clear, confident, and respectful communication. It fosters healthy communication and boundary setting.

→ Unresolved conflicts can cause helplessness and eventually become threats that lead to anger; therefore, it's important to learn healthy conflict resolution.

→ Although conflict resolution can be extremely helpful for anger management, not all issues need to be addressed (internally or externally). Sometimes just giving yourself some time away from stressors and/or using healthy distractions or relaxation techniques can be enough. Just be sure to be aware of any negative emotions that may continue to linger after giving yourself some space from the stressor. If they do linger, it's important to address them.

TAKE IT FORWARD

→ Reflect on your current communication style and journal about it in your anger diary. Consider the following questions:

  → How do you appear to others?

  → Do you have any facial or body tension? Is there tension in your tone?

  → Do people become defensive or feel threatened when you speak up for yourself? Or do they seem calm and open to listening?

  → What are some contributing factors to how they respond to you?

→   Think about the people in your life. Do you feel like they respect your time? Do they respect your boundaries? Can they read your nonverbal communication when you're feeling uncomfortable, irritable, or upset? Journal about this in your anger diary.

→   Try being aware of how clear your communication is. Do you tend to communicate nonverbally or do you clearly state your emotions before becoming angry?

→   Be aware of moments when you feel upset about something that has happened more than once, but you don't speak up until you feel overwhelmed.

People are mostly trying their best, and they deserve the benefit of the doubt. The more I empathize with others, the less angry I will feel.

7

REBUILDING HEALTHY RELATIONSHIPS

Misdirected anger will only cause harm to myself and others. Maintaining healthy relationships is a priority for me, and I will try my best to work with others to manage my anger.

This chapter delves into relationships and how unhealthy anger can affect connections with family, partners, children, and friends. It explains the different ways people with unhealthy anger avoid others, along with the consequences of isolation and how it worsens anger. This chapter also covers ways to repair and improve relationships that have been damaged by anger. The exercises in this chapter will help you learn how to set healthy boundaries, explore damaged relationships, and write an anger agreement.

ANGER AND CONNECTION

Unhealthy anger can affect relationships and connections with partners, children, extended family, and friends. People who suffer from unhealthy anger may have difficulties connecting with others and maintaining relationships. They might limit or avoid social interactions (emotionally, physically, or mentally) or their aggression may drive loved ones away. Aggression can make people feel afraid, confused, or attacked. Some people will still stay around aggressive people regardless, but these relationships are usually not healthy because of the impact of aggression on relationships. Most people will limit their interactions with or avoid people who are aggressive. At the same time, those with unhealthy anger also may limit or avoid interactions with others because they feel ashamed of their anger and want to avoid hurting people. They may be worried about having an outburst, causing conflicts, or being viewed negatively by others.

People with unhealthy anger may isolate emotionally by limiting or avoiding social connections, relying less on others, or hiding their emotions. They may feel that by relying less on others, they have fewer opportunities to feel disappointed or helpless, and therefore a lower chance of becoming angry. They may feel that hiding their emotions will protect them from getting hurt and angry; therefore, they may appear cold and emotionally distant.

People with unhealthy anger may also isolate themselves physically by limiting or avoiding social gatherings. They may immerse themselves in work, or engage in excessive gym time. They may prefer to stay home, limit interactions with loved ones, or communicate through text instead of the phone. They may prefer to live alone, or spend time with their pets instead of people.

People with unhealthy anger may isolate themselves mentally through unhealthy habits such as drinking, using drugs, excessively watching screens, binge eating, or excessively working out. These unhealthy habits may lead to dependence, addiction, weight gain, diabetes, heart issues, liver and lung problems, reduced cognitive functioning, and muscular and physical injuries. They may worsen anxiety, sleep quality, self-esteem, and negative emotions. It's a never-ending cycle of unhealthiness.

Anger leads to isolation and isolation leads to more anger. Connecting with others can break this cycle. When people have healthy relationships, they're more likely to experience positive hormones like endorphins and positive emotions such as love and happiness. Their self-esteem is more likely to improve because they feel loved and accepted. When people experience positive emotions and have healthy self-esteem, they're less likely to become angry and more capable of managing negative emotions in healthy ways. Having a good support system can also help with managing negative emotions because loved ones can provide emotional support and gentle reality checks during moments of irrational thinking. Having people to go to increases the likelihood of reaching out for social support instead of engaging in unhealthy coping skills.

Increased socialization can also provide more opportunities to overcome misunderstandings and other difficult moments that may otherwise lead to anger. The more practice a person has with conflict resolution, the better they will be at it. Healthy relationships allow people the opportunity to replace unhealthy schemas with healthy ones. Unhealthy schemas come from negative experiences and healthy schemas come from positive ones. Over time, with several experiences of not needing to protect oneself, people can feel safe. And this will eventually result in reduced anger.

EXERCISE: ACTIVITY SCHEDULING FOR LOVED ONES

Activity scheduling is a CBT technique that is typically used to treat depression, but can be used to manage unhealthy anger. Scheduling time with people who make you laugh and feel happy and loved will help reduce unhealthy anger. Using the following table as an example, choose your own people, communication modalities, days, and times. Enter these reminders into a physical or digital calendar.

	7AM	10AM	2PM	8PM
SUNDAY		Call _____		
MONDAY		Text _____ to check in		
TUESDAY			Text _____ to check in	
WEDNESDAY				
THURSDAY			Text _____ to check in	
FRIDAY		Call _____		
SATURDAY		Call _____		

EXERCISE: HEALTHY BOUNDARIES

Being able to say no is part of healthy boundary setting, which is one component of being assertive. When people need to set boundaries but don't do so, they allow difficult situations to go on for longer than necessary. This can lead to helplessness, anxiety, and anger. Here you'll find some tips for saying no, followed by a mix-and-match exercise and some fill-ins to practice healthy boundary-setting yourself.

→ Acknowledge the listener's needs so that they feel respected.

→ Say yes somewhere in the message by emphasizing what you can do, as opposed to what you can't.

→ Use positive language as opposed to negative speech.

→ Express vulnerable emotions as opposed to threatening ones like annoyance, anger, irritability, or frustration.

Mix and match and practice healthy boundary setting:

NEGATIVE STATEMENT	HEALTHY BOUNDARY
Can't you see I'm busy?	I really want to hear what you have to say, but I'm so exhausted right now because I didn't sleep well last night.
You're overwhelming me.	I can't help you with that right now because I have a lot on my plate, but I will try to see if I have time later.
Don't talk to me right now.	I've got a lot on my mind so it'll be difficult for me to give this conversation the attention it deserves.
Get away from me.	
You're really pissing me off.	

IMPROVING YOUR RELATIONSHIPS

Improving and maintaining your relationships is an important step in managing your anger because your relationships can actually help you overcome your anger. Although you're working on managing your anger, you will probably still become triggered by certain people. There are ways to manage such situations in a healthy manner without escalation into anger. Likewise, even if your anger has caused distance between you and a loved one, there are ways to repair the relationship. Certain relationships are worth repairing, because the people you choose to have in your life will play a role in determining how successful you are with following through on your anger management. Having positive relationships can help with reducing the chances of becoming angry in the first place. Healthy relationships can have a positive impact on your mood and self-esteem, and can even reduce body tension.

Anger Agreements

It is important to clearly communicate with loved ones about the life changes you're trying to make. It's even more helpful to invite family and friends to make changes together with you. If they agree and follow through, it will strengthen your relationship. You'll feel more supported and you'll likely see changes sooner than if you were to do it alone.

The conversation about working together should involve discussion of schemas and triggers. This will help you both be aware of and sensitive to each other's emotional needs. It should include the communication tools previously mentioned in this workbook, such as assertiveness, agreeing to be honest, and using "I" statements.

It should also include a tool called an "anger agreement." This is an agreement made with a loved one about how you will both respond during moments of anger. It will help you get on the same page so that difficult situations are less likely to escalate. In this agreement, you decide on what to do when one or both of you is feeling triggered or angry. You'll also agree on how and when to communicate your thoughts and feelings, how to resolve issues, and rules for interacting. It's important to discuss these details while you're both calm because it's difficult to communicate clearly and effectively when emotions are running high. Some points to consider adding include avoiding interactions while angry, giving each other space to cool down, and not interrupting or speaking over each other. An anger agreement can reduce the chances of saying or being subjected to hurtful words or actions (which can easily lead to more anger and conflicts).

Repairing Damaged Relationships

The more supportive people you have in your life, the better your anger management will be. Unfortunately, unhealthy anger can push loved ones away. Repairing these relationships is a worthwhile pursuit if they have the potential to positively influence your life. The first step is to offer sincere and detailed apologies for anything hurtful said or done. The next step is to explain the ways in which you're trying to improve your mental and emotional health. You should then explain how you plan on treating them with love and respect. And finally, you should create an anger agreement with them.

Lyla

Lyla, now in her mid-20s, suffers from unhealthy anger. During her childhood, she lived in her older sister Pam's shadow. Pam was six years older and a great student. Lyla didn't do as well in school because of her difficulties concentrating. Because of this, their father favored Pam. He frequently reminded Lyla about how much better Pam was. He made these comments with the hope that they would motivate Lyla into being a better student; instead, they made Lyla feel down about herself and jealous of Pam. Lyla saw herself as dumb and unworthy of her father's love.

When Lyla started dating, she found it difficult to stay in relationships because of jealousy. She always felt there was someone prettier or smarter than she was, and she constantly accused her partners of looking at and talking to other girls, even when there wasn't any proof. Whenever she thought she was being deceived, she would have an anger outburst. Every time she had a new partner, she would bring them home to meet her father. But her father, fed up with meeting so many new partners, kicked her out of the home as soon as she turned 18. She moved in with the partner she had at the time.

This partner also suffered from anger problems. They would argue often over anything her partner did that triggered Lyla's jealousy. If her partner's phone received a notification from an app, Lyla would accuse them of getting a text from a lover. One time, while home with her partner, she gave them a kiss with lipstick on and her partner was grossed out because they didn't like how makeup felt on their face. Lyla became livid because she felt rejected. She started yelling at her partner. They yelled back and then walked away to the bathroom. She followed them and kept yelling through the door. After her partner asked several times for her to stop yelling and give them space, they burst out of the bathroom and choke slammed her. The relationship was over, and Lyla's trust issues only worsened.

Lyla's anger ruined her previous relationships and damaged her current one. Had Lyla tried to improve this relationship before it ended, it would have required steps like talking to her partner about her decision to improve her anger management, getting her partner on board with improving their relationship, and creating an anger agreement between them. She could also have considered describing some of the CBT techniques that she would be using to help her on her journey. This would have allowed her partner to consider using the techniques as well and/or to understand the type of support that Lyla would be needing.

EXERCISE: ANGER AGREEMENT

Ask your loved ones to create anger agreements with you. Be sure the lists are placed somewhere easily accessible to both of you.

If you don't have anyone to work on it with, consider making an anger agreement with yourself. List your schemas, triggers, and healthy ways you'd like to respond to your anger. Some coping techniques include journaling, calling a loved one, engaging in deep-breathing exercises, trying a meditation, or doing chores.

Consider these tips to make your own customized agreements.

→ Agree to not follow each other around if either of us asks for space.

→ Agree to suggest we pause a conversation if we're too angry to communicate or we're not listening to each other.

→ Agree to get back to the conversation within a few hours, or sleep on it to be discussed the next day.

→ Agree to use relaxation techniques and/or reach out to others for advice to cool down while we're taking space.

→ Agree to explore and write down our vulnerable emotions and automatic thoughts.

Anger agreement between:

_____

When either of us is feeling annoyed, irritable, frustrated, or angry, we agree to:

_____

_____

_____

_____

While taking space, we agree to try the following to help us become calm and ready to engage with each other:

_____

_____

_____

_____

EXERCISE: IMPROVING YOUR RELATIONSHIPS

In this exercise, you'll explore ways to establish healthy relationships and repair damaged ones. You'll increase awareness of your schemas that get triggered around certain people. And you'll think about what you can do and say to improve these relationships.

I would like to improve my relationship with: _____

Negative assumptions I make around this person:

_____

_____

Things I can say to let them know I'm aware of and working on changing these assumptions:

_____

_____

Things I can do to improve this relationship:

_____

_____

I would like to improve my relationship with: _____

Negative assumptions I make around this person:

_____

_____

Things I can say to let them know I'm aware of and working on changing these assumptions:

_____

_____

Things I can do to improve this relationship:

_____

_____

I would like to improve my relationship with: _____

Negative assumptions I make around this person:

_____

_____

Things I can say to let them know I'm aware of and working on changing these assumptions:

_____

_____

Things I can do to improve this relationship:

_____

_____

Anger Thermometer

Take a moment for self-care. Are you having any emotional triggers based on the topics covered in this chapter? Any thoughts related to isolating yourself from loved ones because of your anger? Any triggers related to relationships that have been ruined by anger? Did the story bring up any triggers for you? Any triggers related to failed relationships and difficulties managing conflicts?

Write about any triggers here, and if necessary, try the relaxation tip below.

_____

_____

_____

_____

_____

_____

Relaxation Tip: Stretching and Shoulder Rolling

When you're feeling angry, consider stretching as one of your coping techniques. Try these different body movements, but always listen to your body when it comes to these types of exercises.

1. Raise your shoulders, bring them back (as if you're trying to bring your shoulder blades together), then bring them down, forward, and up again. Repeat this circular motion slowly three times.

2. Open your arms wide, with palms open, too, for 10 seconds.

3. Slowly bring your hands up as high as you can. While your hands are high up, gently pull each wrist upward to stretch your upper back muscles for 5 seconds each.

4. Stretch your upper back and arms by bringing your hands together behind your lower back and pulling them away and upward from your body. Hold for 10 seconds.

5. Shift your arms to one side and then to the other for 5 seconds each.

CHAPTER TAKEAWAYS

→ Uncontrolled anger can affect relationships and connections with partners, children, extended family, and friends. People who suffer from unhealthy anger tend to have difficulties connecting with others and/or maintaining relationships.

→ There are several ways people with unhealthy anger might disconnect from loved ones, including mentally, emotionally, and physically. Unhealthy anger can be embarrassing, so many people try to avoid getting triggered.

→ Having more healthy relationships can help with anger management. It's important to have people you can be vulnerable around, so that you can be more in touch with those emotions as opposed to stronger emotions.

→ An anger agreement can help you communicate better with loved ones during moments of anger. In this agreement, you discuss your schemas and triggers, as well as ways you both plan on responding during tense interactions.

→ It might be helpful to repair certain relationships that were damaged by anger, if the people are loving, accepting, and supportive.

TAKE IT FORWARD

→ Be aware of moments when you isolate yourself emotionally, mentally, or physically from others. In your anger diary, write about ways you might be isolating yourself from others.

→ Try to repair any relationships that have been damaged by your anger. Use the content from the exercise about repairing relationships to reach out to a loved one.

→ Follow through on the activity scheduling exercise for connecting with loving and supportive family and friends. Don't be afraid to reach out to loved ones. You don't have to talk to them about what you're going through; just check in and listen to how they're doing.

Relationships with calm, supportive people are worth repairing. If I've hurt someone who is emotionally healthy and willing to help with my healing, I will try to make amends with them.

8

PRACTICING SELF-CARE

Unhealthy anger causes harm to my physical, cognitive, and emotional well-being. I will learn and implement a healthy lifestyle so that I can feel happier.

This chapter focuses on self-care. Anger can take a major toll on the body, so it's important to learn skills to attend to physical needs as well as emotional and mental ones. A healthy lifestyle and engaging in regular self-care activities for the body, mind, and emotions will help you feel less angry. Some of the exercises in the chapter revolve around handling stress, learning self-care, and practicing a relaxing lifestyle.

ANGER'S TOLL ON THE BODY

The fight-or-flight response is meant to be a short-term solution, only to address whatever is threatening safety. Once the threat is gone, the body is supposed to get back to a relaxed state so that it can recharge. In the event that a perceived threat continues to exist and a person still feels angry, the body may continue experiencing the fight-or-flight response. As you can imagine, this will take a toll on the body.

If a stressor that's causing anger continues to exist beyond the initial threat, the stress hormones cortisol and epinephrine are released by the adrenal glands to maintain the fight-or-flight response. This causes prolonged suppression of appetite and the immune system, acceleration of the heart rate, and muscle tension. Continuous release of cortisol can lead to Cushing's disease, which is characterized by high blood pressure, high glucose levels, muscle weakness, fatigue, and weight gain. Continuous release of epinephrine can lead to irritability, jitters, insomnia, anxiety, and weight loss.

Feeling angry most of the time can lead to ongoing fatigue, unhealthy blood sugar levels, heart issues, pain, dental issues, and serious diseases. When the body runs low on energy, it can lead to a weakened immune system because it lacks energy to fight infections. It can cause an increased appetite for fatty and sugary foods as a way to replenish the energy that was lost during the activation of the fight-or-flight response. It can lead to depression and anxiety, which would take a further toll on the body.

The more anger a person experiences, the more their blood sugar rises. Increased glucose in the blood requires more insulin production to move the sugar out of the blood. If insulin production can't keep up with moving the glucose out of the bloodstream, then this can lead to health problems like headaches, fatigue, dry mouth and thirst, nausea and vomiting, frequent urination, blurry vision, and shortness of breath. If there is enough insulin to keep up with the increased amount of glucose from frequent anger, it could lead to more glycogens (a mass form of glucose) in the liver and muscles. If the body doesn't use up enough energy to get rid of the glycogens, then the glycogens could convert to fat for even longer-term storage. This can lead to weight gain and other health issues, like diabetes and problems with the liver, kidneys, and heart.

Frequently experiencing anger can cause heart issues such as angina (chest pain), high blood pressure, damaged blood vessels, heart attacks, strokes, and even death. Unhealthy anger can also cause physical pain: muscle pain from body tension or pain from injuries sustained during an anger episode. It can cause bruxism (teeth grinding) which can result in jaw pain, headaches, tooth pain, and dental issues. It can lead to intentional or impulsive self-harm.

EXERCISE: EXPLORE THE IMPACT OF ONGOING ANGER ON YOUR BODY

Do you relate to any of the health issues described in the previous section? Do you know anyone who suffers from ongoing anger and also deals with any of these issues? Journal about how unhealthy anger has or is affecting your health or that of someone you know.

_____

_____

_____

_____

_____

_____

_____

_____

_____

_____

_____

_____

_____

_____

_____

_____

EXERCISE: SELF-CARE ACTIVITIES

In order to prevent or reduce anger, it's important to take care of your emotional, mental, and physical well-being. In this exercise, you'll explore how you take care of yourself and whether or not these "self-care" activities are healthy. List your self-care activities in the following categories, and whether or not they're healthy. If they're healthy, write about how you can do them more often. If they're not healthy, write about what you can replace them with.

Emotional Well-Being

SELF-CARE ACTIVITY	HEALTHY OR NOT?	HOW I CAN BE MORE CONSISTENT WITH THIS ACTIVITY -OR- WHAT ACTIVITY I CAN REPLACE IT WITH
Ex. Binge watching my favorite TV show for 4 hours	Not	Listening to relaxing music while sitting in a dimly lit room for 10 minutes, following a guided meditation for 15 minutes, doing yoga for 15 minutes, or taking a long bath or shower

Mental Well-Being

SELF-CARE ACTIVITY	HEALTHY OR NOT?	HOW I CAN BE MORE CONSISTENT WITH THIS ACTIVITY -OR- WHAT ACTIVITY I CAN REPLACE IT WITH

Physical Well-Being

SELF-CARE ACTIVITY	HEALTHY OR NOT?	HOW I CAN BE MORE CONSISTENT WITH THIS ACTIVITY -OR- WHAT ACTIVITY I CAN REPLACE IT WITH

Fran and Lara

For five years, Fran worked as a personal assistant for a business owner, Lara, who was very disorganized. Fran never really had an issue with Lara's disorganization because she figured it was part of her job to deal with it. After five years, Fran transitioned to a sales position. Lara's disorganized behavior continued to cause problems, but now it was affecting Fran's sales and commissions. Lara would constantly assign projects and incomplete ideas to Fran and the rest of her staff. Fran would excitedly expand on the ideas and come up with next steps. But when Lara saw that the ideas were not exactly what she had envisioned, she would berate Fran by saying that Fran's ideas were no good and that it was a mistake transitioning Fran to sales. Fran's resentment started to build. She didn't have enough sales experience to move on to another company, so she felt stuck. She continued trying to please Lara with every task and project, but to no avail. When Lara would ask Fran for her opinion on something, Fran would share her opinion and Lara would disregard it. At times, Lara would disregard Fran's ideas but later present them to the team as her own. Fran felt angry about this and took it out on her partner and kids at home. In addition, Fran often found herself stress eating. And during her time working for Lara, she developed health issues, such as insomnia, fatigue, and prediabetes.

One day, Lara asked Fran to host a meeting with another company to present a new product. Fran meticulously prepared the presentation for weeks. The day before the presentation, right before Lara left for the day, she gave Fran a large sheet of paper for Fran to track investors' interest in the product. When Fran looked at it, not only did she see the product she was going to present, but also three other products that she had no knowledge about. This worried Fran immensely, to the point of losing her appetite and sleep. The next day, Fran was on edge from not eating or sleeping, and from anger related to this project. She thought coffee would help, but it only made her more irritable. Not thinking rationally, Fran stormed into Lara's office and started yelling at her. Lara yelled back, and they had a screaming match.

Had Fran attended to her physical, emotional, and mental health, she would have handled her anger differently. She wouldn't have taken her anger out on her family and she would have tried to communicate better at work by using assertiveness and setting healthy boundaries. She could have attended to her physical health by practicing sleep hygiene (healthy bedtime and sleep habits) and having a healthy diet. She could have attended to her emotional health by journaling about her stress daily and seeing a therapist. Her mental well-being could have improved with daily meditation at home and short relaxation breaks (taking walks, deep breathing) while at work.

TAKE TIME FOR YOURSELF

Managing anger and healing the body require focus, and for many, a change in how they treat themselves. Actions that attend to a person's own physical, mental, and emotional well-being are known as "self-care." Self-care reduces the likelihood of becoming angry because it relaxes the mind and body and improves emotional well-being. The further away a person is from physical, mental, and emotional manifestations of anger, the harder it will be for the body to reach an angry state; therefore, engaging in self-care will have a positive effect on emotions and automatic thoughts.

When the body is healthy, the likelihood of experiencing strong negative emotions lessens. Living a healthy lifestyle will typically result in improved mood, increased energy, and a calmer mind.

Diet

Unhealthy foods and beverages contain toxins, such as sweeteners, artificial colors, high amounts of sodium, unhealthy fats, and preservatives. In order for the body to get rid of these toxins, it requires additional insulin and energy. Emotional regulation requires a lot of energy, so when the body uses its energy to get rid of toxins, it robs the brain of the energy necessary to handle upsetting situations. So, in order to have a brain capable of managing anger, it's best to ingest fewer toxins. Healthy foods improve brain functioning, increase energy, strengthen the immune and digestive systems, and help improve overall mood.

Eating a consistently healthy diet, including reducing caffeine and alcohol intake, can help keep anger at bay. Ways to do this include meal prep, avoiding grocery shopping while hungry, using grocery lists and sticking to them, buying more whole foods instead of processed meals, reading labels and only buying foods that have natural ingredients, reducing intake of added sugars and sugar substitutes, practicing mindful eating, and setting time aside and reminders to eat three meals and two healthy snacks per day (or whatever your doctor or nutritionist recommends).

Physical Activity

Physical activity can help improve energy, mood, self-esteem, mental clarity, and sleep quality. It can create happy hormones, make it more likely for you to have a solution-focused mentality, and decrease the chances of becoming angry. It can heal and reduce the chances of developing some chronic diseases. The amount of physical activity a person should engage in depends on the amount of food they ingest. Generally, at least 15 minutes of vigorous exercise per day (or 30 minutes of moderate exercise per day) should be enough, but a physician or nutritionist can provide more information on what specifically will work for each individual. In order to be consistent with physical activity, it's a good idea to try to schedule time out daily for it, and to have any gear necessary for exercise prepared each night before bedtime.

Mental and Emotional Well-Being

Just as physical well-being can help with anger management, so can mental health. Caring for your mind will make it easier to manage negative thinking and emotions. Reducing stimulation and screen time in all settings can help keep a calm mind. An evening routine involving a relaxing ambience can help with winding down after a long day.

Caring for your emotional well-being can reduce negative thoughts. Some ways to improve emotional well-being include journaling throughout the day, connecting with others, and using positive self-talk.

EXERCISE: FUEL YOUR BRAIN
FOR ANGER MANAGEMENT

A healthy body and a good amount of energy are vital for anger management. Many people know this yet they don't get enough water, food, and/or sleep because of difficulties managing time or sticking to routines. Managing your time with regard to meals, snacks, water, and sleep can help you get into a healthy rhythm and reduce anger episodes.

In this exercise, you'll set times to have three meals, two healthy whole-food snacks (or the amount and frequency recommended by your doctor or nutritionist), an eight-ounce glass of water with every meal and snack, one cup as soon as you wake up and another between dinner and bedtime (you'll need more or less depending on how thirsty you are, how dry your skin is, the moisture level in the air, and the amount of fluids you release through bodily fluids), and seven to nine hours of sleep (depending on your needs). If you have a different work schedule every week, you should still be able to schedule these very important routines at the beginning of every week.

TIME	SUNDAY	MONDAY	TUESDAY
7 a.m.		Glass of water	Glass of water
7:45 a.m.		Water/Breakfast	Water/Breakfast
8 a.m.	Glass of water		
8:45 a.m.	Water/Breakfast		
11:30 a.m.	Water/Snack	Water/Snack	Water/Snack
1 p.m.	Water/Lunch	Water/Lunch	Water/Lunch
4 p.m.	Water/Snack	Water/Snack	Water/Snack
7 p.m.	Water/Dinner	Water/Dinner	Water/Dinner
9 p.m.	Glass of water	Glass of water	Glass of water
11 p.m.	Sleep		
12 a.m.		Sleep	Sleep

TIME	SUNDAY	MONDAY	TUESDAY

WEDNESDAY	THURSDAY	FRIDAY	SATURDAY
Glass of water	Glass of water	Glass of water	
Water/Breakfast	Water/Breakfast	Water/Breakfast	
			Glass of water
			Water/Breakfast
Water/Snack	Water/Snack	Water/Snack	Water/Snack
Water/Lunch	Water/Lunch	Water/Lunch	Water/Lunch
Water/Snack	Water/Snack	Water/Snack	Water/Snack
Water/Dinner	Water/Dinner	Water/Dinner	Water/Dinner
Glass of water	Glass of water	Glass of water	Glass of water
			Sleep
Sleep	Sleep	Sleep	

WEDNESDAY	THURSDAY	FRIDAY	SATURDAY

EXERCISE: EXPLORE THE CAUSES OF YOUR FATIGUE OR IRRITABILITY

Exploring the causes of your fatigue can help you target them so that you can improve your energy, and therefore have mental energy for handling upsetting emotions. Describe the following factors that might be contributing to fatigue and/or irritability, and then write down some ways to improve each.

Water intake:

_____

Ways to improve:

_____

Diet/toxin intake:

_____

Ways to improve:

_____

Amount of food:

_____

Ways to improve:

_____

Physical activity:

_____

Ways to improve:

_____

Sleep:

_____

Ways to improve:

_____

Stressors/responsibilities:

_____

Ways to improve:

_____

Keeping worries or angry thoughts on your mind:

_____

Ways to improve:

_____

FIND STRESS RELIEF

Learning ways to alleviate emotional, physical, and mental tension (i.e., stress) can help reduce anger episodes. By minimizing the tension, people can take the time to process thoughts more carefully and choose words and actions that are more likely to result in healthy and productive communication; they can take control over their anger. This section will list some ideas on how to find physical, mental, and emotional comfort, and thereby relieve stress.

Creating happy hormones, such as endorphins and serotonin, can help relieve emotional stress. Some ways to do this include taking a brisk walk or jog, engaging in a brief vigorous workout alone or in a group, dancing, yoga, tai chi, or simple stretching. Other ways to increase endorphins include physical touch (such as hugs or self-hugs, getting a massage or engaging in self-massage), snuggling with something cozy (such as a pet, body pillow, or soft blanket), wearing a plush bathrobe and slippers, taking long warm showers or baths, connecting with loved ones, engaging in favorite hobbies, laughing, listening to music, and creating music or art.

Techniques such as diaphragmatic breathing and meditation will reduce physical stress by reducing the heart rate and relaxing the muscles. There are lots of diaphragmatic breathing exercises, some which are described in this workbook, including square breathing, alternate nostril breathing, left nostril breathing, and 4-7-8 breathing. These are different breathing patterns that ultimately help people feel more relaxed physically and mentally.

Meditation can help manage mental stress because it provides a healthy distraction, slows the heart rate, and can relax the muscles. It is a practice characterized by the combination of mindfulness, breathing, a relaxed body position, something to focus on throughout the practice, and a quiet space with minimal to no distractions. (When trying to relax, it's best to avoid screen time because it can be easy for social media content, a text message, or an email to trigger more negative emotions.) Some meditation types include:

→ Focused meditation, which involves focusing on a specific object or sound. The senses are used to describe in detail everything about the object of focus.

→ Guided meditation, which involves being guided through what you will be visualizing and how you will be breathing. Usually there are relaxing sounds or music in the background.

→ Smiling meditation, which entails smiling during the exhalations.

→ Mantra meditation, in which the participant repeats a verbal or mental mantra (a sound, word, or phrase), with the intention of focusing on it.

→ Progressive relaxation meditation, which requires tensing different muscle groups during the inhalation and then relaxing them during the exhalation.

When people have too much on their plates causing stress, using a CBT technique called "graded task assignment" (breaking down tasks into smaller, manageable subtasks) can help reduce mental stress. Other ways to promote emotional comfort include journaling, repeating self-encouraging affirmations, and reaching out to loved ones or a mental health professional for support.

EXERCISE: GRADED TASK ASSIGNMENT

People often keep to-do lists in their heads, but having too much on the mind can cause anyone to feel overwhelmed, and make it more likely to experience stress, and ultimately, unhealthy anger. Graded task assignment helps reduce stress as well as the chances of becoming angry. Keep in mind that even a task that you perceive as minor could actually be overwhelming.

Practice graded task assignment here:

List a task that you have to get done (whether major or minor):

_____

Now list the subtasks required to get the task done:

_____

_____

_____

If you still feel overwhelmed, continue breaking them down further until the tasks feel manageable.

_____

_____

_____

EXERCISE: ACTIVITY SCHEDULING FOR A RELAXING LIFESTYLE

Taking time for relaxing and positive activities on a daily basis can help keep stress, and anger, at bay. Use the example below for reference to schedule your own relaxing activities.

TIME	SUNDAY	MONDAY	TUESDAY
7 a.m.		10-minute meditation	10-minute meditation
10 a.m.	Full body stretch	Full body stretch	Full body stretch
2 p.m.	Take a 15-minute walk	Take a 15-minute walk	Take a 15-minute walk
8 p.m.	Long bath		

TIME	SUNDAY	MONDAY	TUESDAY

WEDNESDAY	THURSDAY	FRIDAY	SATURDAY
10-minute meditation	10-minute meditation	10-minute meditation	
Full body stretch	Full body stretch	Full body stretch	Full body stretch
Take a 15-minute walk	Take a 15-minute walk	Take a 15-minute walk	Take a 15-minute walk
Long bath			

WEDNESDAY	THURSDAY	FRIDAY	SATURDAY

Anger Thermometer

Take a moment for self-care. Are you having any emotional triggers based on the topics discussed in this chapter? Any thoughts related to an unhealthy lifestyle? Any thoughts related to health issues that might have resulted from anger? Did the story bring up any triggers for you? Any thoughts related to having a stressful work environment? Any feelings related to misdirecting anger toward loved ones or having conflicts with supervisors?

Write about any triggers here, and if necessary, try the relaxation tip below.

_____

_____

_____

Relaxation Tip: 4-7-8 Breathing

4-7-8 breathing can promote deep relaxation and help with falling asleep. It entails inhaling for 4 seconds, holding the breath for 7 seconds, and exhaling for 8 seconds.

1. Start in a relaxed body position, such as sitting or lying down, with feet shoulder-width apart and hands on your lap or by your side.

2. Close your eyes and purse your lips.

3. Start with slowly exhaling while making a "whooshing" sound.

4. Inhale through your nose (or mouth if not possible) for 4 seconds.

5. Hold your breath for 7 seconds.

6. Exhale with pursed lips and while making a whooshing sound for 8 seconds.

7. Repeat four times when you're first getting used to this exercise. With more practice, you can gradually increase the number of cycles to eight.

CHAPTER TAKEAWAYS

→   Repeated episodes of anger can affect the body. Some of the health issues that can result include fatigue, heart issues, blood sugar issues, weight gain, increased appetite for unhealthy foods, and dental issues.

→   Toxins are usually added to processed foods. Emotional regulation requires a lot of energy, so when the body uses its energy to get rid of toxins, it robs the brain of the energy necessary to handle upsetting situations.

→   Healthy foods and regular physical activity improve brain functioning, increase energy, strengthen the immune and digestive systems, and help improve overall mood.

→   Creating happy hormones, such as endorphins and serotonin, through self-care activities can help relieve stress.

→   When trying to relax or get into a positive mindset, it's best to avoid screen time or turn off notifications, because it can be easy for social media content, a text message, or an email to trigger more negative emotions.

TAKE IT FORWARD

→ Eat more home-cooked meals by meal planning and prepping. Create a "menu board" where you'll hang up a binder clip with 4 to 10 index cards containing your favorite easy recipes. Choose days to meal prep and grocery shop, and add reminders on your calendar to do so.

→ Get a large water bottle with markers that can help you track the amount of water you drink, and monitor yourself for dehydration by checking your energy levels, urine frequency and color, and moisture levels in your mouth, on your lips, and on your skin.

→ Practice mindful eating to reduce overeating. Sit at a table with just your food and beverage. Leave your phone in another room on silent mode. Take a bite of food and slowly start moving it around in your mouth, noting changes in textures, temperatures, and flavors. Chew it 10 to 40 times (depending on firmness) until it loses texture. Then swallow. Repeat with another bite of food.

Healthy food has the fuel I need to manage my negative emotions. I will prioritize my physical well-being in order to reduce the chances of becoming angry.

9

MANAGING ANGER FOR THE LONG-TERM

*I can and will be able to manage my anger.
I'm capable of expressing my strong negative
emotions calmly, using words and a soft, calm
tone of voice.*

This chapter will explore long-term resolutions for managing unhealthy anger. There are so many reasons to be hopeful, and the information and exercises in this workbook along with other avenues of healing, also explored here, should prepare you for long-term success. The exercises in this chapter will give you the opportunity to take personal responsibility, complete a CBT thought record, create a "coping skills toolbox," and reflect upon the next steps on your journey.

YOU'RE IN CONTROL

Managing anger takes practice, patience, and persistence. There will be many ups and downs.

If you're feeling like your anger is getting out of control again, reread this book and work through some of the exercises again. If you feel like you would benefit from more support or find that there are barriers to following through with some of the suggestions in this book, you may consider talking to a mental health professional. Keep in mind that vulnerable emotions and underlying mental health issues may be getting in the way of managing your anger. Therefore, you may need to address them in order to resolve your anger. Remember to involve supportive people in your journey. Having the right support will increase your likelihood of success. Consider repairing some relationships that have been damaged by anger. Improve the way you communicate your emotions and needs and practice assertiveness. Use CBT cognitive restructuring to improve your schemas and automatic thoughts and reduce your anger triggers.

Always be mindful of the fact that if you aren't well physically, you likely won't be well emotionally. Routines, reminders, and activity scheduling will be vital for your success. Adding reminders for health-related activities (including annual physical checkups) to your calendar and referring to your calendar frequently throughout the day can help with establishing a healthy lifestyle. Here are some tips on establishing healthy routines for anger management success.

Set aside a weekly day and time to plan out your meals for the week. If you can eat the same breakfast and lunch during work days, it might be easier to prepare a large amount of ingredients at the beginning of the week. You can look up easy and healthy recipes or ask around for recommendations. Be sure to schedule out time for leisure activities, time with others (over the phone or in person), and time for physical activities. Not moving enough can cause body tension, and this can increase the chances of the fight-or-flight system being activated during stressful moments.

Many people use substances to relieve stress. Although some can help in the moment, once the substance is no longer in the body, irritability and stress may return. This may lead to substance dependence or abuse, which can cause issues with functioning in different areas of one's life. If you use healthy coping strategies to control your anger, you won't need substances to control it for you.

In order to keep up with the techniques, use your support system. Involving family, friends, support groups, communities, and mental health professionals will help you stay consistent with the healthy coping and communication skills you've learned here.

EXERCISE: TAKING PERSONAL RESPONSIBILITY/ REDUCE BLAMING OTHERS

When it comes to anger management, taking personal responsibility will help set you free. Personal responsibility isn't "blaming." It's accepting that you take part in situations and aren't a victim, because seeing yourself as a victim will only worsen your anger. In the following statements, practice finding the personal responsibility, the blaming schema, and healthy actions you can take to feel empowered.

Example:

Statement: My partner cheated on me.

Blaming/angry schema: My partner is a terrible person.

Personal responsibility: There's no guarantee of loyalty in relationships. I chose to take the risk of being cheated on when I entered this relationship.

Healthy actions I can take: End the relationship, ask my partner to address their issues in their own therapy, go to individual or couples counseling to resolve the trust issues.

Statement: My coworker keeps dismissing my ideas.

Blaming/angry schema:

_____

Personal responsibility:

_____

Healthy actions I can take:

_____

Statement: I went on two interviews last week and both jobs emailed me with rejection letters.

Blaming/angry schema:

_____

Personal responsibility:

_____

Healthy actions I can take:

_____

Statement: My child doesn't listen when I ask them to do something.

Blaming/angry schema:

_____

Personal responsibility:

_____

Healthy actions I can take:

_____

EXERCISE: CBT THOUGHT RECORD

A thought record is a CBT journaling tool used for processing strong negative emotions, automatic thoughts, schemas, evidence that proves and disproves schemas, and balanced thoughts. It's a chart with seven columns and can be used whenever a person experiences strong negative emotions. The purpose is to identify schemas, distinguish fact from opinion, and reduce the intensity of negative emotions.

Although this tool can be helpful for mitigating intense emotions, it does take a lot of practice to be able to use it properly. One challenging part of this exercise is discerning between opinion and fact, because sometimes opinions can feel like facts. It can also be difficult to identify or admit to your schemas. Negative schemas are strong and undesirable beliefs, so people usually want to avoid them or deny that they exist.

Follow the instructions and read through the examples on page 158–159 to practice your own thought record.

Instructions:

1. Start with filling in the situation column. This should be a brief description of what triggered your anger.

2. In the second column, list emotions and ratings from 1 to 10, with 1 meaning the emotion doesn't exist and 10 meaning the emotion is extremely intense.

3. Select the strongest emotion. If there is more than one emotion with the same high rating, choose the one you prefer to focus on. Circle or highlight it.

4. In the third column, explore your automatic thoughts related to the strongest emotion.

5. Use the downward arrow technique to explore the schema. Remember that schemas are the deep underlying beliefs you have about yourself, others, the world, and the future.

6. Circle or highlight the schema.

7. In the "Evidence for" column, list the facts that prove the schema to be true.

8. In the "Evidence against" column, list the facts that go against the schema.

9. In the "Balanced Thoughts" column, start with "although," then list one statement from the "evidence for" column, write in a comma, and list a statement from the "Evidence against" column. If possible, try to match statements from each column. Sometimes you won't have something to match. In these cases, you can add a true statement that fits well.

10. Take some time to reflect on the balanced thoughts. How much do you believe them to be true? If you don't believe them to be true, then they need to be rewritten to reflect facts.

11. In the last column, relist the emotions from column 2 and rerate them (1 to 10, with 0 meaning you no longer feel the emotion and 10 meaning the emotion is extremely intense) based on how you feel after completing the thought record. If you have new emotions, you can list them here.

SITUATION	EMOTIONS AND RATINGS (1 TO 10)	AUTOMATIC THOUGHTS AND SCHEMA	EVIDENCE FOR	
My parents showed up unannounced	**Angry—8** Confused—5 Disrespected—7	They're rude. They're entitled. ↓ **They don't respect me.**	They showed up unannounced, without respect for my time. They don't follow my rules for the kids when they're with them.	

	EVIDENCE AGAINST	BALANCED THOUGHTS	RELIST AND RERATE EMOTIONS + NEW EMOTIONS
	They don't question my life choices. They often tell me what a great parent I am.	Although they showed up unannounced without respect for my time, they respect me enough to not question my life choices. Although they don't follow my rules for the kids, they often tell me what a great parent I am.	Angry—5 Confused—5 Disrespected—5

Les

Les, 45, is 9-year-old Ben's parent. Les suffers from anger issues related to parenting. Les often feels overwhelmed and lost with regard to his son's behavior. Ben complains every time he needs to get homework done, doesn't do as he is told, interrupts others when they speak, and always gets up from the dinner table in the middle of his meal. He knows the rules: No complaining, get all homework done, listen to his parents, don't interrupt people when they speak, and stay in the seat until the meal is finished.

Les feels that he isn't asking for much. As a child, there were many more expectations of him, like doing chores. In addition, whenever he broke the rules, he would get hit. He feels this was an effective way to parent, and wishes he could hit Ben as a form of discipline. But he worries that doing so will get him in trouble with child protective services. So, Les screams at Ben instead.

One day, Ben was sitting at the table trying to get his homework done. He was unable to focus, so he started tapping his pencil on the table, looking at the ceiling and squirming around. Les yelled at him to get his work done. This startled Ben

SITUATION	EMOTIONS AND RATINGS (1 TO 10)	AUTOMATIC THOUGHTS AND SCHEMA	EVIDENCE FOR	
I asked Ben to take out the trash in his room an hour ago, but he's playing in his room instead.	**Angry—10** Confused—6 Disrespected—8	He thinks he can do whatever he wants. ↓ He doesn't respect my authority.	He often doesn't do as he is told. He often doesn't listen to me.	

into doing his work quickly but carelessly. After dinner, Les reminded Ben to brush his teeth and get ready for bed. Ben went to brush his teeth but got distracted by their dog on the way to the bathroom. He got down on the floor to pet the dog for a while, then started making the dog do tricks. Then he returned to his room and started playing. Les considered Ben to be disrespectful because he didn't do as he was told. Les came into Ben's room, yelling and calling him disrespectful and a bad son.

Ben's teacher informs Les that Ben does not do his schoolwork, he bothers his peers, he doesn't sit still, and he interrupts his teachers and peers when they speak. Les thinks of Ben as rude. Les becomes angry because this is not behavior that Ben learned at home. Les feels stressed and angry. Les compares Ben to his older sister who is responsible, does as she is told, and gets all her schoolwork done. When Les tries to talk to Ben about these issues, Ben interrupts him and goes off on tangents, losing track of the conversation's focus. Les feels disrespected and disconnected, and resents time spent with Ben because it's exhausting. In order to process these negative emotions, Les could use CBT thought records like the following one.

	EVIDENCE AGAINST	BALANCED THOUGHTS	RELIST AND RERATE EMOTIONS + NEW EMOTIONS
	He gets his chores done when I supervise him and keep him on track. He comes to me immediately when he hears me calling.	Although he often doesn't do as he is told, he gets his chores done when I supervise him and keep him on track. Although he often doesn't listen to me, he comes to me immediately when he hears me calling.	Angry—4 Confused—7 Disrespected—0 Sad—4

WHAT TO DO IF YOUR ANGER
IS STILL A PROBLEM

In addition to using the information and strategies in this workbook, there are other important avenues for healing. I hope that the information and workbook exercises here help you get started on your healing journey from all the pain that anger has caused you. I hope that they've helped increase your insight into your anger, schemas, and triggers. I hope they help you start the process of mending broken relationships and improving current ones. And I hope you've learned some healthy coping and communication skills that you will use during moments of anger and beyond.

But you don't have to continue this anger journey alone. There are ways to get help, including through mental health professionals, support groups, family and friends, and supportive online communities. Having a healthy support system will help you become more aware of your anger. Getting the empathy that you might not have gotten as a child can help you heal from the wounds that have resulted in your anger. Hearing stories from others can help you feel solidarity and become more aware of behaviors you want to avoid or implement.

Work with a Therapist

If you haven't already started therapy with a professional who specializes in anger management, I encourage you to do so. Having weekly or biweekly check-ins can be helpful to:

→   Have a safe space to process angry thoughts

→   Remind you of healthy coping skills to try

→   Hold you accountable for implementing healthy coping skills

→   Address any issues underlying your anger, including depression, anxiety, and trauma

→   Encourage you to get your annual checkups and be aware of your physical health

→   Help you be aware of any decline in your functioning and correlations with irritability or anger

There are lots of different types of therapists, and many who specialize in anger management. Consider whether you want online or in-person therapy. If in person, consider the location. Is the office close to your home or office? Think about whether or not you care about a therapist's gender identity, ethnicity, race, or age. You may feel more comfortable speaking to an older therapist because of their life experience. You may feel more comfortable speaking to a therapist around your age range who might relate more to you. If you've experienced or witnessed "big T" traumas such as neglect, physical abuse, sexual abuse, or assault, you may consider asking your therapist if they specialize or have experience treating patients who have survived such traumas.

In addition, you should ask the therapist what type of approach they use, in order to see if it's a modality that you're interested in trying (e.g., CBT). Another question to ask is how direct or gentle they are. Some people prefer a completely honest and direct approach; others prefer a more gentle and compassionate approach, and still others want a mix of the two. And finally, consider the cost. If you have health insurance, does the therapist accept your insurance? If paying out of pocket, are their rates affordable for you? You can find a therapist by calling your insurance company, searching for a "psychotherapist," "CBT therapist," or "anger management therapist" on your insurance company's website, searching on Psychologytoday.com or Zocdoc.com, or asking for recommendations from people you know.

Sometimes people find the right match with the first therapist they meet and feel instantly connected during the first session. Other times, it takes a few sessions to feel comfortable or it's just not a good fit. Try to be patient with this process because it could take time to find the right person. In addition, if there's something you didn't like about your therapist's words or behavior, speak up. You can always comment on their behavior and words if they made you feel uncomfortable or upset. It's good practice to speak up about your needs and seek clarification during sessions. In fact, therapy is one of the safest spaces to do so.

Support Groups

People who suffer from unhealthy anger often don't have healthy support systems. By attending support groups, they can meet others who are working on their anger. Interacting with these individuals can be helpful for solidarity and to develop a sense of community. When looking for a support group, consider whether you want to attend online or in person, the age of the facilitator and age range of the group members, the location (if in person), and the cost. Consider attending a meeting a few times to feel it out. Ask yourself the following questions: Are group members talking over one another? Is the facilitator allowing everyone a chance to speak? How well does the facilitator manage the group and conflicts among members? Are people mostly empathetic or mostly aggressive? How big is the group?

To find a group, consider conducting a search online for "anger management support group." If you're looking for an in-person group, also add in your city or zip code. You'll find several resources for meetings. You can also search on the *Psychology Today* website or look for an Emotions Anonymous (EA) meeting on the American Addiction Centers website (Recovery.org). EA is a 12-step support group for people dealing with negative emotions such as anger, depression, anxiety, low self-esteem, and grief. Sometimes referred to as "Anger Management Anonymous," this program applies the 12-step approach from Alcoholics Anonymous.

Family and Friends

Whenever possible and helpful, you should try to use the support of family and friends. Think about any past or current friends and family members who are calm, caring, and open communicators. First, reach out to ask them how they're doing. Ask if they have some time to talk about something important. Explain that you realize that your anger is a problem and that you're trying to work on it. Inform them about other supports you're connected to, such as a therapist, a support group, online communities, or other loved ones. This is an important detail that will assure them that you're not trying to rely solely on them for support. Ask if they will consider joining your support team. If so, explain the ways in which they can help. For example, they can help you become aware of times when your tone is aggressive or demeaning. They can inform you verbally or with nonverbal cues. Together, you can decide on the specific words, body language, or gestures they could use to let you know that they're noticing aggression.

Online Communities

There are several online communities for anger management. You can find them by searching online and through social media platforms, such as Facebook, Reddit, or Quora. There is a Facebook group called "Anger Management Support Group" with over 24,000 members. You can search for the group's title on Facebook or type in this link: Facebook.com/groups/angermanagementsupport. There is also a subreddit about anger on Reddit.com/r/Anger. This has a similar purpose, which is to vent about anger management stories and issues, and provide mutual support to those looking for it.

EXERCISE: COPING SKILLS TOOLBOX

A "coping skills toolbox" is a collection of techniques that help a person cope with anger and other negative emotions. It can include:

→ Positive schemas or mantras to tackle negative thoughts when they come up

→ Relaxation techniques

→ Mental and emotional health reminders

→ Actual tools you can use to manage stress, like a diary and pen or sketchbook and pencil

→ Comfort items, like a stuffed toy, stress ball, or relaxing essential oils

This toolbox should be kept easily accessible so that it can be used during difficult moments. The collection can be kept as:

→ A list on a white board or a smartphone's notes app

→ On index cards in an actual box or on a tack board

→ A space on a wall with sticky notes

List your main takeaways and favorite exercises from this workbook to get your toolbox started.

_____

_____

_____

_____

_____

_____

_____

EXERCISE: NEXT STEPS

Think about your next steps after completing this book. What will you do to continue to move forward in your healing process and maintain the skills you learned?

_____

_____

_____

_____

_____

_____

_____

_____

_____

_____

_____

_____

_____

EXERCISE: ANGER SELF-ASSESSMENT

Now that you've completed the workbook, take a moment to revisit the impact of unhealthy anger on your life. Circle the number that corresponds to your answer for each statement, tally up your score, and then look at the score interpretation at the bottom.

Quiz: How Much Does Anger Affect Your Life?

STATEMENT	NEVER	RARELY	SOMETIMES	OFTEN
I'm able to get past my moments of anger in a short period of time.	4	3	2	1
I get tense muscles and/or body aches.	1	2	3	4
I communicate well with others.	4	3	2	1
I have anger outbursts.	1	2	3	4
I respond, rather than react, to my anger.	4	3	2	1
I feel embarrassed as a result of my anger reactions.	1	2	3	4
I eat unhealthy foods or drinks after episodes of anger.	1	2	3	4
I sleep well, regardless of my anger.	4	3	2	1
I throw items during moments of anger.	1	2	3	4
I start arguments and/or fights.	1	2	3	4
I scare people with my anger reactions.	1	2	3	4
Before expressing my anger, I use healthy coping techniques to calm down.	4	3	2	1
People openly disagree with me without fear of getting yelled at.	4	3	2	1
I can be in the present moment, regardless of my anger.	4	3	2	1

Score total _____

SCORE INTERPRETATION:

14 to 28: Your anger doesn't affect your life much, but there is always room for improvement.

29 to 43: Your anger issues affect your life sometimes. You would benefit from some support and anger management techniques.

44 to 56: Anger affects your life a great deal. There's a lot to learn about your anger triggers, as well as ways to regulate and communicate your emotions.

Anger Thermometer

Take a moment for self-care. Are you having any emotional triggers based on the topics discussed in this chapter?

Write about any triggers here, and if necessary, try the relaxation tip below.

_____

_____

Relaxation Tip: Visualization through Art (or Journaling)

Visualization can help get your mind off of negative thoughts and instead focus on a positive, calm, and happy place for a moment. Think about your "happy place" in detail. Now sketch it, along with every detail, including people, animals, textures, smells, sounds, etc. Try using coloring pencils or crayons to help describe moods and other intangible aspects of your happy place.

If you prefer not to sketch, describe it in detail:

_____

_____

_____

_____

CHAPTER TAKEAWAYS

→ If you aren't well physically, you likely won't be well emotionally. Many people know the steps they need to take to be healthy, but they don't follow through consistently. Routines, reminders, and activity scheduling will be vital for your success.

→ The CBT thought record can be a helpful tool to mitigate intense emotions. It does take a lot of practice to be able to use it properly, however.

→ Anger management therapy can be helpful in many ways. Therapy is confidential and the vast majority of therapists are nonjudgmental. A therapist can be a safe person with whom to share your anger. A CBT therapy session can give you the opportunity and encouragement to utilize CBT tools.

→ When you involve family and friends in a healthy way, you set yourself up for success. Loved ones can help you with managing your anger because they see you from a more objective point of view than you see yourself.

→ Many people suffering from anger management issues feel lonely. Joining support groups and online communities will help you feel connected to others and will give you a healthy outlet for your anger.

TAKE IT FORWARD

→   Look into the online anger management communities. Read through some of the stories. Comment if you have some empathetic thoughts. Note how it feels to offer support to others who are going through similar experiences. Consider joining and/or using these resources.

→   Now that you've decided how you want to format your coping skills toolbox, it's time to create it. Use the graded task assignment technique to break down this task into subtasks and then schedule some time to get the subtasks done.

→   If you haven't already and you feel it would be helpful, find a therapist. Check with your insurance to see what might be covered and find out if you have a copay or coinsurance. For an explanation of insurance terminology, you can use this website: HealthCare.gov/blog/understand-health-insurance-definitions (or search online for "health insurance explained").

I will learn to use healthy coping strategies to mitigate my anger and stress. I will use my resources to create a solid anger management team.

Resources

To understand more about the brain on anger: *Healing the Angry Brain: How Understanding the Way Your Brain Works Can Help You Control Anger and Aggression* by Ronald T. Potter-Efron

Information on how the brain works and how to change the way yours works: *Rewire: Change Your Brain to Break Bad Habits, Overcome Addictions, Conquer Self-Destructive Behavior* by Richard O'Connor

Relaxation techniques: NCCIH.NIH.gov/health/relaxation-techniques-what-you -need-to-know

Sleep recommendations and information: SleepFoundation.org

More information on CBT: *Cognitive Behavior Therapy, Third Edition: Basics and Beyond* by Judith S. Beck

Guidelines from the CDC on physical activity for health: CDC.gov/physicalactivity /basics/adults/index.htm

Tips for healthy communication skills: *Active Listening Techniques: 30 Practical Tools to Hone Your Communication Skills* by Nixaly Leonardo, LCSW

A guided journal with anger management techniques: *Anger Management Journal: Identify Your Triggers, Change Your Outlook, and Manage Your Emotions* by Nixaly Leonardo, LCSW

Online anger management classes:

AngerManagementOnline.com

AngerManagementSeminar.com

AngerMasters.com

MentalHealth.OpenPathCollective.org/anger-management/free-class

Online anger management supportive communities:

Facebook.com/groups/angermanagementsupport

Reddit.com/r/Anger

In-person anger management groups:

Call Emotions Anonymous 888-997-6780 or visit their website:
Recovery.org/support-groups/emotions-anonymous

Search for a group on Psychology Today's website:
PsychologyToday.com/us/groups/anger-management

Apps to help with anger management:

Calm

CBT Thought Diary

Gratitude: Journal App

Happify: For Stress & Worry

Relax Melodies

References

AbuHasan, Qais, Vamsi Reddy, and Waquar Siddiqui. "Neuroanatomy, Amygdala." In StatPearls [Internet]. Treasure Island, FL: StatPearls Publishing, 2021. NCBI.NLM.NIH.gov/books /NBK537102.

"Adrenaline." HealthDirect. Last reviewed April 2021. HealthDirect.gov.au/adrenaline.

Cirino, Erica. "Chewing Your Food: Is 32 Really the Magic Number?" Healthline. Updated March 18, 2020. Healthline.com/health/how-many-times-should-you-chew-your-food#benefits.

"Dehydration." MedlinePlus. Updated July 28, 2021. MedlinePlus.gov/dehydration.html.

Denson, Thomas F., William C. Pedersen, Jacyln Ronquillo, and Anirvan S. Nandy. "The Angry Brain: Neural Correlates of Anger, Angry Rumination, and Aggressive Personality." *Journal of Cognitive Neuroscience* 21, no. 4 (2009): 734–44. doi.org/10.1162/jocn.2009.21051.

DeRubeis, Robert J., Greg J. Siegle, and Steven D. Hollon. "Cognitive Therapy vs. Medications for Depression: Treatment Outcomes and Neural Mechanisms. *Nature Reviews Neuroscience* 9, no. 10 (October 2008) 788–96. doi: 10.1038/nrn2345.

Fuhrman, Joel. "The Hidden Dangers of Fast and Processed Food." *American Journal of Lifestyle Medicine* 12, no. 5 (September–October 2018): 375–81. doi: 10.1177/1559827618766483.

"Get the Facts about TBI." Centers for Disease Control and Prevention. Last reviewed May 12, 2021. CDC.gov/traumaticbraininjury/get_the_facts.html.

Gotter, Ana. "What Is the 4–7-8 Breathing Technique?" Healthline. Updated April 20, 2018. Healthline.com/health/4-7-8-breathing#Other-techniques-to-help-you-sleep.

Harmon-Jones, E., & Allen, J. J. B. Anger and Frontal Brain Activity: EEG Asymmetry Consistent with Approach Motivation Despite Negative Affective Valence. *Journal of Personality and Social Psychology* 74, no. 5 (1998): 1310–16. doi.org/10.1037/0022-3514.74.5.1310.

Hart, Tessa, Jo Ann Brockway, Jesse R. Fann, Roland D. Maiuro, and Monica J. Vaccaro. "Anger Self-Management in Chronic Traumatic Brain Injury: Protocol for a Psycho-educational Treatment with a Structurally Equivalent Control and an Evaluation of Treatment Enactment." *Contemporary Clinic Trials* 40 (January 2015) 180–92. doi: 10.1016/j.cct.2014.12.005.

"Hyperglycemia (High Blood Glucose)." American Diabetes Association. Accessed September 17, 2021. Diabetes.org/healthy-living/medication-treatments/blood-glucose-testing -and-control/hyperglycemia.

Joyner, Michael J., and Darren P. Casey "Regulation of Increased Blood Flow (Hyperemia) to Muscles during Exercise: A Hierarchy of Competing Physiological Needs." *Physiological Reviews* 95, no. 2 (April 2015): 549–601. doi: 10.1152/physrev.00035.2013.

Lee, Do Yup, Eosu Kim, and Man Ho Choi. "Technical and Clinical Aspects of Cortisol as a Biochemical Marker of Chronic Stress. *BMB Reports* 48, no. 4 (April 2015): 209–16. doi: 10.5483/BMBRep.2015.48.4.275.

Ma, Xiao, Zi-Qi Yue, Zhu-Qing Gong, Hong Zhang, Nai-Yue Duan, Yu-Tong Shi, Gao-Xia Wei, and You-Fa Li. "The Effect of Diaphragmatic Breathing on Attention, Negative Affect and Stress in Healthy Adults." *Frontiers in Psychology* 8 (2017): 874. doi: 10.3389/fpsyg.2017.00874.

"Manage Blood Sugar." Centers for Disease Control and Prevention. Last reviewed April 28, 2021. CDC.gov/diabetes/managing/manage-blood-sugar.html.

"Meditation: In Depth." National Center for Contemporary Integrative Health. Last updated April 2016. NCCIH.NIH.gov/health/meditation-in-depth.

Mouri, Mouri, and Madhu Badireddy. "Hyperglycemia." In StatPearls [Internet]. Treasure Island, FL: StatPearls Publishing, 2021. NCBI.NLM.NIH.gov/books/NBK430900.

Nunez, Kirsten. "Fight, Flight, Freeze: What This Response Means." Healthline. February 21, 2020. healthline.com/health/mental-health/fight-flight-freeze.

Ohira, Tetsuya, Hiroyasu Iso, Takeshi Tanigawa, Tomoko Sankai, Hironori Imano, Masahiko Kiyama, Shinichi Sato, Yoshihiko Naito, Minoru Iida, and Takashi Shimamoto. "The Relation of Anger Expression with Blood Pressure Levels and Hypertension in Rural and Urban Japanese Communities. *Journal of Hypertension* 20, no. 1 (January 2002): 21–7. doi: 10.1097/00004872-200201000-00005.

Pal, Gopal Krushna, Ankit Agarwal, Shanmugavel Karthik, Pravati Pal, and Nivedita Nanda. "Slow Yogic Breathing through Right and Left Nostril Influences Sympathovagal Balance, Heart Rate Variability, and Cardiovascular Risks in Young Adults." *National American Journal of Medical Sciences* 6, no. 3 (March 2014): 145–51. doi: 10.4103/1947-2714.128477.

Pirau, Letitia, and Forshing Lui. "Frontal Lobe Syndrome." In StatPearls [Internet]. Treasure Island, FL: StatPearls Publishing, 2021. NCBI.NLM.NIH.gov/books/NBK532981.

Potter-Efron, Ronald. *Healing the Angry Brain: How Understanding the Way Your Brain Works Can Help You Control and Anger and Aggression.* 1st ed. Oakland, CA: New Harbinger Publications, 2012.

Preckela, Daniel, and Roland von Känel. "Regulation of Hemostasis by the Sympathetic Nervous System: Any Contribution to Coronary Artery Disease?" *Heartdrug* 4, no. 3 (2004): 123–30. doi: 10.1159/000078415.

Rao, Vani, Paul Rosenberg, Melaine Bertrand, Saeed Salehinia, Jennifer Spiro, Sandeep Vaishnavi, Pramit Rastogi, Kathy Noll, David J. Schretlen, Jason Brandt, Edward Cornwell, Michael Makley, and Quincy Samus Miles. "Aggression After Traumatic Brain Injury: Prevalence and Correlates." *The Journal of Neuropsychiatry and Clinical Neurosciences* 21, no. 4 (2009): 420–9. doi: 10.1176/jnp.2009.21.4.420.

Raypole, Crystal. "13 Ways to Increase Endorphins." Healthline. September 27, 2019. Healthline.com/health/how-to-increase-endorphins.

Rnic, Katerina, David J. A. Dozois, and Rod A. Martin. "Cognitive Distortions, Humor Styles, and Depression." *Europe's Journal of Psychology* 12, no. 3 (August 2016): 348–62. doi: 10.5964/ejop.v12i3.1118.

Saghir, Zahid, Javeria N. Syeda, Adnan S. Muhammad, Tareg H. Balla Balla Abdalla. "The Amygdala, Sleep Debt, Sleep Deprivation, and the Emotion of Anger: A Possible Connection?" *Cureus* 10, no. 7 (July 2018): e2912. doi: 10.7759/cureus.2912.

"Skin Blushing/Flushing." MedlinePlus. Last updated October 8, 2021. MedlinePlus.gov/ency/article/003241.htm.

Steffgen, Georges. "Anger Management—Evaluation of a Cognitive-Behavioral Training Program for Table Tennis Players." *Journal of Human Kinetics* 55 (January 2017): 65–73. doi: 10.1515/hukin-2017-0006.

Suni, Eric. "Bruxism: Teeth Grinding at Night." Sleep Foundation. Updated September 23, 2021. SleepFoundation.org/bruxism.

Taggart, Peter, Mark R. Boyett, Sunil Jit R. J. Logantha, and Pier D. Lambiase. "Anger, Emotion, and Arrhythmias: from Brain to Heart." *Frontiers in Psychology* 2 (2011): 67. doi: 10.3389/fphys.2011.00067.

Undas, Anetta, Ilona Wiek, Ewa Stêpien, Krzysztof Zmudka, and WiesławaTracz. "Hyperglycemia Is Associated with Enhanced Thrombin Formation, Platelet Activation, and Fibrin Clot Resistance to Lysis in Patients with Acute Coronary Syndrome." *Diabetes Care* 31, no. 8 (August 2008): 1590–95. doi: 10.2337/dc08-0282.

Vorvick, Linda J. "Relaxation Techniques for Stress." MedlinePlus. Last reviewed August 13, 2020. MedlinePlus.gov/ency/patientinstructions/000874.htm.

Index

mental health, 137

    physical activity, 136–137, 147, 152

    scheduling, 137–139, 144–145

    stress relief, 141–143

Self-esteem, 83–84, 86

Self-massage, 17

Serotonin, 142, 147

Should statements, 51

Smiling meditation, 67

Solution-focused

    mentality, 77, 91–92

Soothing sounds, 85

Square breathing, 108

Stress relief, 141–143, 147

Stretching, 125–126

Substance use, 152

Support groups, 152, 161–162, 167

Sympathetic nervous system

    (SNS), 8, 72

T

Therapists, 24, 160–161, 167, 168

Thought records, 154–157, 167

Thoughts

    automatic, 13, 22, 25–26, 32, 42–43

    balanced, 28–29, 54–55, 57, 68, 69

    negative, 50–51

Threats

    actual vs. imagined, 2

    emotional, 2

    perceived, 2, 8, 18

    physical, 2

Trauma, 36–37, 46

Traumatic brain injury (TBI), 37

Triggers, 42–45, 46–47

V

Visualization, 64, 166–167

ACKNOWLEDGMENTS

Thanks to my family and friends for your inspiration on my anger stories. Special thanks to my husband for all those times you helped me get through my writer's block. Another special thanks to my parents, sister, and cousins (especially Kenia and Yessi) for your overwhelming support!

ABOUT THE AUTHOR

 **Nixaly Leonardo, LCSW,** was born and raised in New York City by immigrant parents, along with her older brother and younger sister. She is a wife and a mother of two. She is a Licensed Clinical Social Worker and CBT therapist. She has over 10 years of experience helping clients with anger management, depression, anxiety, PTSD, ADHD, parenting, and interpersonal problems. She's written books about communication skills and anger management, and plans to write many more in order to help as many people as possible. For more information, visit PracticalOnlineTherapy.com.